FREE DVD  FREE DVD

## *From Stress to Success* DVD from Trivium Test Prep

Dear Customer,

Thank you for purchasing from Trivium Test Prep! Whether you're a new teacher or looking to advance your career, we're honored to be a part of your journey.

To show our appreciation (and to help you relieve a little of that test-prep stress), we're offering a **FREE *SAT II Math Level 1 Essential Test Tips DVD***\* by Trivium Test Prep. Our DVD includes 35 test preparation strategies that will help keep you calm and collected before and during your big exam. All we ask is that you email us your feedback and describe your experience with our product. Amazing, awful, or just so-so: we want to hear what you have to say!

To receive your **FREE *SAT II Math Level 1 Essential Test Tips DVD***, please email us at 5star@ triviumtestprep.com. Include "Free 5 Star" in the subject line and the following information in your email:

1. The title of the product you purchased.
2. Your rating from 1 – 5 (with 5 being the best).
3. Your feedback about the product, including how our materials helped you meet your goals and ways in which we can improve our products.
4. Your full name and shipping address so we can send your **FREE *SAT II Math Level 1 Essential Test Tips DVD***.

If you have any questions or concerns please feel free to contact us directly at 5star@triviumtestprep.com.

Thank you, and good luck with your studies!

\* Please note that the free DVD is not included with this book. To receive the free DVD, please follow the instructions above.

# SAT II Math Level 1 Subject Test Study Guide 2021-2022

## Comprehensive Review with Practice Test Questions for the SAT II Mathematics Level 1 Exam

# TABLE OF CONTENTS

# INTRODUCTION

Congratulations on choosing to take the SAT Mathematics Level 1 Subject Test! By purchasing this book, you've taken an important step on your path to college.

This guide will provide you with a detailed overview of the SAT Mathematics Level 1 Subject Test so that you know exactly what to expect on test day. We'll take you through all the concepts covered on the test and give you the opportunity to test your knowledge with practice questions. Even if it's been a while since you last took a major test, don't worry; we'll make sure you're more than ready!

## What are the SAT Subject Tests?

The SAT Subject Tests measure high school-level aptitude in a given subject and are designed to allow college applicants to showcase their academic strengths in the admissions process. All of the SAT Subject Tests are voluntary, although some colleges may require applicants to complete certain exams, particularly if they are pursuing a specific course of study. More typically, applicants choose the tests that best highlight their strengths and areas of interest. This can be especially helpful for applicants who have studied a subject outside of the classroom, generally through summer or weekend programs, an online course, or independent study.

SAT Subject Test scores are sent to the colleges of the applicant's choosing and are included in his or her application. Some colleges also use the Subject Tests to place students in appropriate courses. At some colleges, high scores can even be used to earn credits or fulfill basic academic requirements.

## What's on the SAT Mathematics Level 1 Subject Test?

The SAT Mathematics Level 1 Subject Test gauges high school-level content knowledge in mathematics, based on two years of algebra and one of geometry. Test-takers are expected to demonstrate mastery of fundamental concepts and skills in mathematics, including numbers and operations, algebra and functions, geometry and measurement, data analysis, statistics, and probability. You will have sixty minutes to answer fifty multiple choice questions.

| SUBJECT | PERCENTAGE |
|---|---|
| Number and Operations | 10 – 14% |
| Algebra and Functions | 38 – 42% |
| Plane Euclidean Geometry | 18 – 22% |
| Coordinate Geometry | 8 – 12% |
| Three-Dimensional Geometry | 4 – 6% |
| Trigonometry | 6 – 8% |
| Data Analysis, Statistics, and Probability | 8 – 12% |
| Total | 60 minutes |

NUMBER AND OPERATIONS: Students must demonstrate knowledge of the various operations, as well as ratio and proportion. In addition you will be asked to work with complex numbers and matrices and demonstrate mastery of sequences, counting, and elementary number theory.

ALGEBRA AND FUNCTIONS: Students must demonstrate knowledge of basic algebraic concepts including expressions, equations, and inequalities. You also will be expected to be able to represent and model algebraic expressions and equations. Finally, the test will assess your mastery of the properties of different types of functions: linear, polynomial, rational, and exponential.

GEOMETRY AND MEASUREMENT: Students must demonstrate mastery of the various topics in geometry, including plane Euclidean, coordinate, and three-dimensional. In coordinate geometry, the test will assess your understanding of lines, parabolas, and circles, and you will be asked to solve problems involving symmetry and transformations. You also must be able to accurately calculate measurements of both two-dimensional and three-dimensional shapes, including cylinders, cones, pyramids, spheres, and prisms. Finally, you will be asked to demonstrate knowledge of trigonometry, including the properties of right triangles and identities.

DATA ANALYSIS, STATISTICS, AND PROBABILITY: Students must demonstrate mastery of basic data analysis and the key concepts in statistics. You must be able to calculate the mean, median, mode, range, and interquartile range of a series of numbers. You must also be able to interpret and depict data through graphs and plots. You will also be asked to complete least squares regression (linear). Finally, you must be able to calculate basic probabilities.

# How is the SAT Mathematics Level 1 Subject Test Scored?

Each multiple-choice question is worth one raw point. The total number of questions you answer correctly is added up to obtain your raw score. A fraction of a point is subtracted for wrong answers: one-quarter of a point for five-choice questions, one-third of a point for four-choice questions, and one-half of a point for three-choice questions. If your final raw score is a fraction, it will be rounded to the nearest whole number. If you are not sure of the answer to a question and you cannot narrow the answers down to two choices, you should skip the question and leave the answer blank, rather than risk losing a fraction of a point to an incorrect answer. This is because no points are deducted for questions left unanswered.

Your raw score is converted to a scaled score ranging from 200 to 800 points. The score relates to a percentile which compares how you did to all other students who took the test. For more information you can check with the College Board website. Colleges and scholarship programs that you preselected to receive your score are informed. They will consider your true ability as approximately forty points higher than your actual score.

You will receive your scores on your SAT Mathematics Level 1 approximately four to six weeks after your test date. For the most current information, check with the College Board. If you select colleges in advance or within nine days following your test date, you can send up to four score reports for free. After that time frame or for reports beyond the first four, each report is twelve dollars. A fee waiver is available. You can also choose which test scores (of tests that have already been scored) are sent to each college using Score Choice™.

# How is the SAT Mathematics Level 1 Subject Test Administered?

The SAT Mathematics Level 1 test is offered six times each school year, in October, November, December, January, May, and June. The test is only offered on days and at locations where the SAT is offered, but not on ALL days that the SAT is offered. You may take the SAT Mathematics Level 1 Subject Test the same day as up to two other Subject Tests, but you cannot take the SAT and SAT Subject Tests on the same day. Check https://collegereadiness.collegeboard.org/sat-subject-tests/register/test-dates-deadlines for more information.

You will need to print your admission ticket from your online account and bring it, along with your identification, to the testing site on test day. You must also bring two No. 2 pencils with erasers. It is also recommended that you bring a watch (without an alarm), a drink or snacks for your break, and a bag or backpack, which you will leave in a locker. You may bring an approved calculator into the testing room. It can be either a scientific or a graphing calculator, although a graphing calculator is recommended. Check with the College Board for the most current information. Make sure your calculator is in good working order before you arrive at the test. You may not share calculators during the test, and the testing center will not provide you with a substitute calculator. During the test, you will be provided a reference sheet including basic volume and area formulas for three-dimensional shapes. No outside printed or written materials or electronic devices (besides a basic watch and your calculator) are allowed in the testing room. You may retake the test on any subsequent testing date.

# About This Guide

This guide will help you master the most important test topics and develop critical test-taking skills. We have built features into our books to prepare you for your tests and increase your score. Along with a detailed summary of the test's format, content, and scoring, we offer an in-depth overview of the content knowledge required to pass the test. In the content review sections, you'll find sidebars that provide interesting information, highlight key concepts, and review content so that you can solidify your understanding of the material that you will be tested on. You can also test your knowledge with sample questions throughout the text and practice questions that reflect the content and format of the SAT Mathematics Level 1 Subject Test. We're pleased you've chosen Accepted, Inc. to be a part of your college journey!

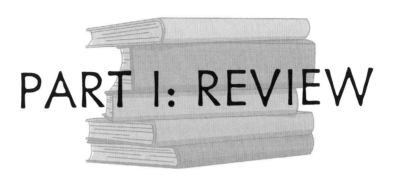

# PART I: REVIEW

# one

# NUMBERS AND OPERATIONS

This chapter provides a review of the basic yet critical components of mathematics such as manipulating fractions, comparing numbers, and using units. These concepts will provide the foundation for more complex mathematical operations in later chapters.

## Types of Numbers

Numbers are placed in categories based on their properties.

- A NATURAL NUMBER is greater than 0 and has no decimal or fraction attached. These are also sometimes called counting numbers {1, 2, 3, 4, ...}.

- WHOLE NUMBERS are natural numbers and the number 0 {0, 1, 2, 3, 4, ...}.

- INTEGERS include positive and negative natural numbers and 0 {..., –4, –3, –2, –1, 0, 1, 2, 3, 4, ...}.

- A RATIONAL NUMBER can be represented as a fraction. Any decimal part must terminate or resolve into a repeating pattern. Examples include –12, $-\frac{4}{5}$, 0.36, $7.\overline{7}$, $26\frac{1}{2}$, etc.

- An IRRATIONAL NUMBER cannot be represented as a fraction. An irrational decimal number never ends and never resolves into a repeating pattern. Examples include $-\sqrt{7}$, $\pi$, and 0.34567989135...

- A REAL NUMBER is a number that can be represented by a point on a number line. Real numbers include all the rational and irrational numbers.

- An IMAGINARY NUMBER includes the imaginary unit $i$, where $i = \sqrt{-1}$ Because $i^2 = -1$, imaginary numbers produce a negative value when squared. Examples of imaginary numbers include $-4i$, $0.75i$, $i\sqrt{2}$ and $\frac{8}{3}i$.

◆ A **COMPLEX NUMBER** is in the form $a + bi$, where $a$ and $b$ are real numbers. Examples of complex numbers include $3 + 2i$, $-4 + i$, $\sqrt{3} - i\sqrt[3]{5}$ and $\frac{5}{8} - \frac{7i}{8}$. All imaginary numbers are also complex.

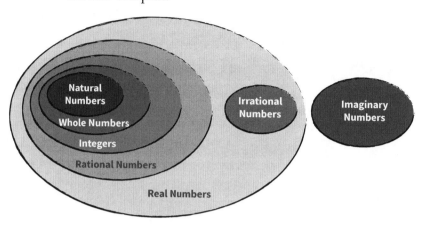

**Figure 1.1. Types of Numbers**

The **FACTORS** of a natural number are all the numbers that can multiply together to make the number. For example, the factors of 24 are 1, 2, 3, 4, 6, 8, 12, and 24. Every natural number is either prime or composite. A **PRIME NUMBER** is a number that is only divisible by itself and 1. (The number 1 is not considered prime.) Examples of prime numbers are 2, 3, 7, and 29. The number 2 is the only even prime number. A **COMPOSITE NUMBER** has more than two factors. For example, 6 is composite because its factors are 1, 6, 2, and 3. Every composite number can be written as a unique product of prime numbers, called the **PRIME FACTORIZATION** of the number. For example, the prime factorization of 90 is $90 = 2 \times 3^2 \times 5$. All integers are either even or odd. An even number is divisible by 2; an odd number is not.

## Properties of Number Systems

A system is **CLOSED** under an operation if performing that operation on two elements of the system results in another element of that system. For example, the integers are closed under the operations of addition, subtraction, and multiplication but not division. Adding, subtracting, or multiplying two integers results in another integer. However, dividing two integers could result in a rational number that is not an integer $\left(-2 \div 3 = \frac{-2}{3}\right)$.

◆ The rational numbers are closed under all four operations (except for division by 0).

◆ The real numbers are closed under all four operations.

◆ The complex numbers are closed under all four operations.

◆ The irrational numbers are NOT closed under ANY of the four operations.

If a real number is a natural number (e.g., 50), then it is also a whole number, an integer, and a rational number.

The **COMMUTATIVE PROPERTY** holds for an operation if order does not matter when performing the operation. For example, multiplication is commutative for integers: $(-2)(3) = (3)(-2)$.

The **ASSOCIATIVE PROPERTY** holds for an operation if elements can be regrouped without changing the result. For example, addition is associative for real numbers: $-3 + (-5 + 4) = (-3 + -5) + 4$.

The **DISTRIBUTIVE PROPERTY** of multiplication over addition allows a product of sums to be written as a sum of products: $a(b + c) = ab + ac$. The value $a$ is distributed over the sum $(b + c)$. The acronym FOIL (First, Outer, Inner, Last) is a useful way to remember the distributive property.

When an operation is performed with an **IDENTITY ELEMENT** and another element $a$, the result is $a$. The identity element for multiplication on real numbers is $a \times 1 = a$), and for addition is 0 ($a + 0 = a$).

An operation of a system has an **INVERSE ELEMENT** if applying that operation with the inverse element results in the identity element. For example, the inverse element of $a$ for addition is $-a$ because $a + (-a) = 0$. The inverse element of $a$ for multiplication is $\frac{1}{a}$ because $a \times \frac{1}{a} = 1$.

---

## EXAMPLES

1) Classify the following numbers as natural, whole, integer, rational, or irrational. (The numbers may have more than one classification.)

   **A.** 72

   **B.** $-\frac{2}{3}$

   **C.** $\sqrt{5}$

   Answers:

   A. The number is **natural, whole**, an **integer**, and **rational**.

   B. The fraction is **rational**.

   C. The number is **irrational**. (It cannot be written as a fraction, and written as a decimal is approximately 2.2360679...)

2) Determine the real and imaginary parts of the following complex numbers.

   **A.** 20

   **B.** $10 - i$

   **C.** $15i$

   Answers:

   A complex number is in the form of $a + bi$, where $a$ is the real part and $bi$ is the imaginary part.

   A. $20 = 20 + 0i$
      **The real part is 20, and there is no imaginary part.**

B. $10 - i = 10 - 1i$

**The real part is 10, and –1i is the imaginary part.**

C. $15i = 0 + 15i$

**The real part is 0, and the imaginary part is 15i.**

3) Answer True or False for each statement:

    **A.** The natural numbers are closed under subtraction.

    **B.** The sum of two irrational numbers is irrational.

    **C.** The sum of a rational number and an irrational number is irrational.

**Answers:**

    A. **False**. Subtracting the natural number 7 from 2 results in $2 - 7 = -5$, which is an integer, but not a natural number.

    B. **False**. For example, $(5 - 2\sqrt{3}) + (2 + 2\sqrt{3}) = 7$. The sum of two irrational numbers in this example is a whole number, which is not irrational. The sum of a rational number and an irrational number is sometimes rational and sometimes irrational.

    C. **True**. Because irrational numbers have decimal parts that are unending and with no pattern, adding a repeating or terminating decimal will still result in an unending decimal without a pattern.

4) Answer true or false for each statement:

    **A.** The associative property applies for multiplication in the real numbers.

    **B.** The commutative property applies to all real numbers and all operations.

**Answers:**

    A. **True**. For all real numbers, $a \times (b \times c) = (a \times b) \times c$. Order of multiplication does not change the result.

    B. **False**. The commutative property does not work for subtraction or division on real numbers. For example, $12 - 5 = 7$, but $5 - 12 = -7$, and $10 \div 2 = 5$, but $2 \div 10 = \frac{1}{5}$.

# Operations with Complex Numbers

Operations with complex numbers are similar to operations with real numbers in that complex numbers can be added, subtracted, multiplied, and divided. When adding or subtracting, the imaginary parts and real parts are combined separately. When multiplying, the distributive property (FOIL) can be applied. Note that multiplying complex numbers often creates the value $i^2$ which can be simplified to –1.

To divide complex numbers, multiply both the top and bottom of the fraction by the COMPLEX CONJUGATE of the divisor (bottom number). The complex conjugate is the complex number with the sign of the imaginary part changed. For example, the complex conjugate of 3 + 4$i$ would be 3 − 4$i$. Since both the top and the bottom of the fraction are multiplied by the same number, the fraction is really just being multiplied by 1. When simplified, the denominator of the fraction will now be a real number.

## EXAMPLES

**1)** Simplify: $(3 − 2i) − (−2 + 8i)$

**Answer:**

| | |
|---|---|
| $(3 − 2i) − (−2 + 8i)$ | |
| $= (3 − 2i) − 1(−2 + 8i)$ $= 3 − 2i + 2 − 8i$ | Distribute the −1. |
| $= \mathbf{5 − 10i}$ | Combine like terms. |

**2)** Simplify: $\dfrac{4i}{(5 − 2i)}$

**Answer:**

| | |
|---|---|
| $\dfrac{4i}{(5 − 2i)}$ | |
| $= \dfrac{4i}{5 − 2i}\left(\dfrac{5 + 2i}{5 + 2i}\right)$ $= \dfrac{20i + 8i^2}{25 + 10i − 10i − 4i^2}$ | Multiply the top and bottom of the fraction by the complex conjugate of 5 + 2$i$. |
| $= \dfrac{20i + 8(−1)}{25 + 10i − 10i − 4(−1)}$ $= \dfrac{20i − 8}{25 + 10i − 10i + 4}$ | Simplify the result using the identity $i^2 = −1$. |
| $= \dfrac{20i − 8}{29}$ | Combine like terms. |
| $= \dfrac{−8}{29} + \dfrac{20}{29}i$ | Write the answer in the form $a + bi$. |

# Scientific Notation

**SCIENTIFIC NOTATION** is a method of representing very large and small numbers in the form $a \times 10^n$, where $a$ is a value between 1 and 10, and $n$ is a nonzero integer. For example, the number 927,000,000 is written in scientific notation as $9.27 \times 10^8$. Multiplying 9.27 by 10 eight times gives 927,000,000. When performing operations with scientific notation, the final answer should be in the form $a \times 10^n$.

When adding and subtracting numbers in scientific notation, the power of 10 must be the same for all numbers. This results in like terms in which the $a$ terms are added or subtracted and the $10^n$ remains unchanged. When multiplying numbers in scientific notation, multiply

65000000.
7 6 5 4 3 2 1
↓
$6.5 \times 10^7$

.0000987
-1-2-3-4-5
↓
$9.87 \times 10^{-5}$

**Figure 1.2. Scientific Notation**

When multiplying numbers in scientific notation, add the exponents. When dividing, subtract the exponents.

the $a$ factors, and then multiply that answer by 10 to the sum of the exponents. For division, divide the $a$ factors and subtract the exponents.

## EXAMPLES

1) Simplify: $(3.8 \times 10^3) + (4.7 \times 10^2)$

**Answer:**

| | |
|---|---|
| $(3.8 \times 10^3) + (4.7 \times 10^2)$ | |
| $3.8 \times 10^3 = 3.8 \times 10 \times 10^2 = 38 \times 10^2$ | To add, the exponents of 10 must be the same. |
| $38 \times 10^2 + 4.7 \times 10^2 = 42.7 \times 10^2$ | Add the $a$ terms together. |
| $\mathbf{= 4.27 \times 10^3}$ | Write the number in proper scientific notation. |

2) Simplify: $(8.1 \times 10^{-5})(1.4 \times 10^7)$

**Answer:**

| | |
|---|---|
| $(8.1 \times 10^{-5})(1.4 \times 10^7)$ | |
| $8.1 \times 1.4 = 11.34$ $-5 + 7 = 2$ $= 11.34 \times 10^2$ | Multiply the $a$ factors and add the exponents on the base of 10. |
| $\mathbf{= 1.134 \times 10^3}$ | Write the number in proper scientific notation. |

# Order of Operations

The **order of operations** is simply the order in which operations are performed. **PEMDAS** is a common way to remember the order of operations:

1. Parentheses
2. Exponents
3. Multiplication
4. Division
5. Addition
6. Subtraction

Multiplication and division, and addition and subtraction, are performed together from left to right. So, performing multiple operations on a set of numbers is a four-step process:

1. P: Calculate expressions inside parentheses, brackets, braces, etc.
2. E: Calculate exponents and square roots.
3. MD: Calculate any remaining multiplication and division in order from left to right.
4. AS: Calculate any remaining addition and subtraction in order from left to right.

Always work from left to right within each step when simplifying expressions.

## EXAMPLES

**1)** Simplify: $2(21 - 14) + 6 \div (-2) \times 3 - 10$

**Answer:**

| | |
|---|---|
| $2(21 - 14) + 6 \div (-2) \times 3 - 10$ | |
| $= 2(7) + 6 \div (-2) \times 3 - 10$ | Calculate expressions inside parentheses. |
| $= 14 + 6 \div (-2) \times 3 - 10$ <br> $= 14 + (-3) \times 3 - 10$ <br> $= 14 + (-9) - 10$ | There are no exponents or radicals, so perform multiplication and division from left to right. |
| $= 5 - 10$ <br> $= -5$ | Perform addition and subtraction from left to right. |

**2)** Simplify: $-(3)^2 + 4(5) + (5 - 6)^2 - 8$

**Answer:**

| | |
|---|---|
| $-(3)^2 + 4(5) + (5 - 6)^2 - 8$ | |
| $= -(3)^2 + 4(5) + (-1)^2 - 8$ | Calculate expressions inside parentheses. |
| $= -9 + 4(5) + 1 - 8$ | Simplify exponents and radicals. |
| $= -9 + 20 + 1 - 8$ | Perform multiplication and division from left to right. |
| $= 11 + 1 - 8$ <br> $= 12 - 8$ <br> $= 4$ | Perform addition and subtraction from left to right. |

**3)** Simplify: $\dfrac{(7 - 9)^3 + 8(10 - 12)}{4^2 - 5^2}$

**Answer:**

| | |
|---|---|
| $\dfrac{(7 - 9)^3 + 8(10 - 12)}{4^2 - 5^2}$ | |
| $= \dfrac{(-2)^3 + 8(-2)}{4^2 - 5^2}$ | Calculate expressions inside parentheses. |
| $= \dfrac{-8 + (-16)}{16 - 25}$ | Simplify exponents and radicals. |
| $= \dfrac{-24}{-9}$ | Perform addition and subtraction from left to right. |
| $= \dfrac{8}{3}$ | Simplify. |

# Units of Measurement

The standard units for the metric and American systems are shown below, along with the prefixes used to express metric units.

Table 1.1. Units and Conversion Factors

| Dimension | American | SI |
| --- | --- | --- |
| length | inch/foot/yard/mile | meter |
| mass | ounce/pound/ton | gram |
| volume | cup/pint/quart/gallon | liter |
| force | pound-force | newton |
| pressure | pound-force per square inch | pascal |
| work and energy | cal/British thermal unit | joule |
| temperature | Fahrenheit | kelvin |
| charge | faraday | coulomb |

Table 1.2. Metric Prefixes

| Prefix | Symbol | Multiplication Factor |
| --- | --- | --- |
| tera | T | 1,000,000,000,000 |
| giga | G | 1,000,000,000 |
| mega | M | 1,000,000 |
| kilo | k | 1,000 |
| hecto | h | 100 |
| deca | da | 10 |
| base unit | -- | -- |
| deci | d | 0.1 |
| centi | c | 0.01 |
| milli | m | 0.001 |
| micro | μ | 0.000001 |
| nano | n | 0.000000001 |
| pico | p | 0.000000000001 |

A mnemonic device to help remember the metric system is *King Henry Drinks Under Dark Chocolate Moon* (KHDUDCM).

Units can be converted within a single system or between systems. When converting from one unit to another unit, a conversion factor (a numeric multiplier used to convert a value with a unit to another unit) is used. The process of converting between units using a conversion factor is sometimes known as dimensional analysis.

Table 1.3. Conversion Factors

| | |
|---|---|
| 1 in. = 2.54 cm | 1 lb. = 0.454 kg |
| 1 yd. = 0.914 m | 1 cal = 4.19 J |
| 1 mi. = 1.61 km | $1\,°F = \frac{9}{5}\,°C + 32\,°C$ |
| 1 gal. = 3.785 L | $1\,cm^3 = 1\,mL$ |
| 1 oz. = 28.35 g | 1 hr = 3600 s |

## EXAMPLES

1) Convert the following measurements in the metric system.

   **A.** 4.25 kilometers to meters

   **B.** $8\,m^2$ to $mm^2$

   **Answers:**

   A. $4.25\,km \left( \frac{1000\,m}{1\,km} \right) =$ **4250 m**

   B. $\frac{8\,m^2}{1} \times \frac{1000\,mm}{1\,m} \times \frac{1000\,mm}{1\,m} =$ **8,000,000 mm²**

   Since the units are square units ($m^2$), multiply by the conversion factor twice, so that both meters cancel.

2) Convert the following measurements in the American system.

   **A.** 12 feet to inches

   **B.** $7\,yd^2$ to $ft^2$

   **Answers:**

   A. $12\,ft \left( \frac{12\,in}{1\,ft} \right) =$ **144 in**

   B. $7\,yd^2 \left( \frac{3ft^2}{1yd^2} \right) \left( \frac{3ft^2}{1yd^2} \right) =$ **63 ft²**

   Since the units are square units ($ft^2$), multiply by the conversion factor twice.

3) Convert the following measurements in the metric system to the American system.

   **A.** 23 meters to feet

   **B.** $10\,m^2$ to $yd^2$

   **Answers:**

   A. $23\,m \left( \frac{3.28\,ft}{1\,m} \right) =$ **75.44 ft**

   B. $\frac{10\,m^2}{1} \times \frac{1.094\,yd}{1\,m} \times \frac{1.094\,yd}{1\,m} =$ **11.97 yd²**

# Fractions

A FRACTION is a number that can be written in the form $\frac{a}{b}$, where $b$ is not equal to 0. The $a$ part of the fraction is the NUMERATOR (top number) and the $b$ part of the fraction is the DENOMINATOR (bottom number).

If the denominator of a fraction is greater than the numerator, the value of the fraction is less than 1 and it is called a PROPER FRACTION (for example, $\frac{3}{5}$ is a proper fraction). In an IMPROPER FRACTION, the denominator is less than the numerator and the value of the fraction is greater than 1 ($\frac{8}{3}$ is an improper fraction). An improper fraction can be written as a MIXED NUMBER, which has a whole number part and a proper fraction part. Improper fractions can be converted to mixed numbers by dividing the numerator by the denominator, which gives the whole number part, and the remainder becomes the numerator of the proper fraction part. (For example, the improper fraction $\frac{25}{9}$ is equal to mixed number $2\frac{7}{9}$ because 9 divides into 25 two times, with a remainder of 7.)

Conversely, mixed numbers can be converted to improper fractions. To do so, determine the numerator of the improper fraction by multiplying the denominator by the whole number, and then adding the numerator. The final number is written as the (now larger) numerator over the original denominator.

To convert mixed numbers to improper fractions:
$$a\frac{m}{n} = \frac{n \times a + m}{n}$$

Fractions with the same denominator can be added or subtracted by simply adding or subtracting the numerators; the denominator will remain unchanged. To add or subtract fractions with different denominators, find the LEAST COMMON DENOMINATOR (LCD) of all the fractions. The LCD is the smallest number exactly divisible by each denominator. (For example, the least common denominator of the numbers 2, 3, and 8 is 24.) Once the LCD has been found, each fraction should be written in an equivalent form with the LCD as the denominator.

To multiply fractions, the numerators are multiplied together and denominators are multiplied together. If there are any mixed numbers, they should first be changed to improper fractions. Then, the numerators are multiplied together and the denominators are multiplied together. The fraction can then be reduced if necessary. To divide fractions, multiply the first fraction by the reciprocal of the second.

Any common denominator can be used to add or subtract fractions. The quickest way to find a common denominator of a set of values is simply to multiply all the values together. The result might not be the least common denominator, but it will allow the problem to be worked.

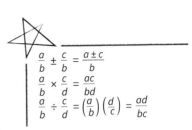

$$\frac{a}{b} \pm \frac{c}{b} = \frac{a \pm c}{b}$$
$$\frac{a}{b} \times \frac{c}{d} = \frac{ac}{bd}$$
$$\frac{a}{b} \div \frac{c}{d} = \left(\frac{a}{b}\right)\left(\frac{d}{c}\right) = \frac{ad}{bc}$$

## EXAMPLES

**1)** Simplify: $2\frac{3}{5} + 3\frac{1}{4} - 1\frac{1}{2}$

**Answer:**

$2\frac{3}{5} + 3\frac{1}{4} - 1\frac{1}{2}$

| | |
|---|---|
| $= 2\frac{12}{20} + 3\frac{5}{20} - 1\frac{10}{20}$ | Change each fraction so it has a denominator of 20, which is the LCD of 5, 4, and 2. |
| $2 + 3 - 1 = 4$ <br> $\frac{12}{20} + \frac{5}{20} - \frac{10}{20} = \frac{7}{20}$ | Add and subtract the whole numbers together and the fractions together. |
| $4\frac{7}{20}$ | Combine to get the final answer (a mixed number). |

**2)** Simplify: $\frac{7}{8} \times 3\frac{1}{3}$

**Answer:**

$\frac{7}{8} \times 3\frac{1}{3}$

| | |
|---|---|
| $3\frac{1}{3} = \frac{10}{3}$ | Change the mixed number to an improper fraction. |
| $\frac{7}{8}\left(\frac{10}{3}\right) = \frac{7 \times 10}{8 \times 3}$ <br> $= \frac{70}{24}$ | Multiply the numerators together and the denominators together. |
| $= \frac{35}{12}$ <br> $= 2\frac{11}{12}$ | Reduce the fraction. |

**3)** Simplify: $4\frac{1}{2} \div \frac{2}{3}$

**Answer:**

$4\frac{1}{2} \div \frac{2}{3}$

| | |
|---|---|
| $4\frac{1}{2} = \frac{9}{2}$ | Change the mixed number to an improper fraction. |

| | |
|---|---|
| $\frac{9}{2} \div \frac{2}{3}$ $= \frac{9}{2} \times \frac{3}{2}$ $= \frac{27}{4}$ | Multiply the first fraction by the reciprocal of the second fraction. |
| $= 6\frac{3}{4}$ | Simplify. |

# Ratios

A RATIO is a comparison of two numbers and can be represented as $\frac{a}{b}$, $a:b$, or $a$ to $b$. The two numbers represent a constant relationship, not a specific value: for every $a$ number of items in the first group, there will be $b$ number of items in the second. For example, if the ratio of blue to red candies in a bag is 3:5, the bag will contain 3 blue candies for every 5 red candies. So, the bag might contain 3 blue candies and 5 red candies, or it might contain 30 blue candies and 50 red candies, or 36 blue candies and 60 red candies. All of these values are representative of the ratio 3:5 (which is the ratio in its lowest, or simplest, terms).

To find the "whole" when working with ratios, simply add the values in the ratio. For example, if the ratio of boys to girls in a class is 2:3, the "whole" is five: 2 out of every 5 students are boys, and 3 out of every 5 students are girls.

### EXAMPLES

1) There are 10 boys and 12 girls in a first-grade class. What is the ratio of boys to the total number of students? What is the ratio of girls to boys?

**Answer:**

| | |
|---|---|
| number of boys: 10 number of girls: 12 number of students: 22 | Identify the variables. |
| number of boys : number of students $= 10 : 22$ $= \frac{10}{22}$ $= \frac{5}{11}$ | Write out and simplify the ratio of boys to total students. |
| number of girls : number of boys $= 12 : 10$ $= \frac{12}{10}$ $= \frac{6}{5}$ | Write out and simplify the ratio of girls to boys. |

**2)** A family spends $600 a month on rent, $400 on utilities, $750 on groceries, and $550 on miscellaneous expenses. What is the ratio of the family's rent to their total expenses?

**Answer:**

| | |
|---|---|
| rent = 600<br><br>utilities = 400<br><br>groceries = 750<br><br>miscellaneous = 550<br><br>total expenses = 600 + 400 + 750 + 550 = 2300 | Identify the variables. |
| rent : total expenses<br><br>= 600 : 2300<br><br>$= \frac{600}{2300}$<br><br>$= \frac{6}{23}$ | Write out and simplify the ratio of rent to total expenses. |

# Proportions

A **PROPORTION** is an equation which states that two ratios are equal. A proportion is given in the form $\frac{a}{b} = \frac{c}{d}$, where the $a$ and $d$ terms are the extremes and the $b$ and $c$ terms are the means. A proportion is solved using cross-multiplication ($ad = bc$) to create an equation with no fractional components. A proportion must have the same units in both numerators and both denominators.

## EXAMPLES

**1)** Solve the proportion for $x$: $\frac{3x-5}{2} = \frac{x-8}{3}$.

**Answer:**

| | |
|---|---|
| $\frac{(3x-5)}{2} = \frac{(x-8)}{3}$ | |
| $3(3x-5) = 2(x-8)$ | Cross-multiply. |
| $9x - 15 = 2x - 16$<br><br>$7x - 15 = -16$<br><br>$7x = -1$<br><br>$x = -\frac{1}{7}$ | Solve the equation for $x$. |

**2)** A map is drawn such that 2.5 inches on the map equates to an actual distance of 40 miles. If the distance measured on the map between two cities is 17.25 inches, what is the actual distance between them in miles?

**Answer:**

| | |
|---|---|
| $\dfrac{2.5}{40} = \dfrac{17.25}{x}$ | Write a proportion where $x$ equals the actual distance and each ratio is written as inches : miles. |
| $2.5x = 690$ <br> $x = 276$ <br> The two cities are **276 miles apart**. | Cross-multiply and divide to solve for $x$. |

**3)** A factory knows that 4 out of 1000 parts made will be defective. If in a month there are 125,000 parts made, how many of these parts will be defective?

**Answer:**

| | |
|---|---|
| $\dfrac{4}{1000} = \dfrac{x}{125,000}$ | Write a proportion where $x$ is the number of defective parts made and both ratios are written as defective : total. |
| $1000x = 500,000$ <br> $x = 500$ <br> There are **500 defective parts** for the month. | Cross-multiply and divide to solve for $x$. |

# Percentages

A **PERCENT** (or percentage) means per hundred and is expressed with a percent symbol (%). For example, 54% means 54 out of every 100. A percent can be converted to a decimal by removing the % symbol and moving the decimal point two places to the left, while a decimal can be converted to a percent by moving the decimal point two places to the right and attaching the % sign. A percent can be converted to a fraction by writing the percent as a fraction with 100 as the denominator and reducing. A fraction can be converted to a percent by performing the indicated division, multiplying the result by 100, and attaching the % sign.

The equation for finding percentages has three variables: the part, the whole, and the percent (which is expressed in the equation as a decimal). The equation, as shown below, can be rearranged to solve for any of these variables.

- part = whole × percent
- percent = $\dfrac{\text{part}}{\text{whole}}$
- whole = $\dfrac{\text{part}}{\text{percent}}$

This set of equations can be used to solve percent word problems. All that's needed is to identify the part, whole, and/or percent, and then to plug those values into the appropriate equation and solve.

---

### EXAMPLES

**1)** Change the following values to the indicated form:

  **A.** 18% to a fraction

  **B.** $\frac{3}{5}$ to a percent

  **C.** 1.125 to a percent

  **D.** 84% to a decimal

**Answers:**

  A. The percent is written as a fraction over 100 and reduced: $\frac{18}{100} = \frac{9}{50}$.

  B. Dividing 5 by 3 gives the value 0.6, which is then multiplied by 100: **60%**.

  C. The decimal point is moved two places to the right: $1.125 \times 100 =$ **112.5%**.

  D. The decimal point is moved two places to the left: $84 \div 100 =$ **0.84**.

**2)** In a school of 650 students, 54% of the students are boys. How many students are girls?

**Answer:**

| | |
|---|---|
| Percent of students who are girls = 100% − 54% = 46% | |
| percent = 46% = 0.46 | Identify the variables. |
| whole = 650 students | |
| part = ? | |
| part = whole × percent<br>= 0.46 × 650 = 299<br>**There are 299 girls.** | Plug the variables into the appropriate equation. |

---

## Percent Change

Percent change problems involve a change from an original amount. Often percent change problems appear as word problems that include discounts, growth, or markups. In order to solve percent change problems, it's necessary to identify the percent change (as a decimal), the amount of change, and the original amount. (Keep in mind that one of these will be the value being solved for.) These values can then be plugged into the equations below:

- amount of change = original amount × percent change

Key terms associated with percent change problems include discount, sales tax, and markup.

- percent change = $\dfrac{\text{amount of change}}{\text{original amount}}$
- original amount = $\dfrac{\text{amount of change}}{\text{percent change}}$

## EXAMPLES

1) An HDTV that originally cost $1,500 is on sale for 45% off. What is the sale price for the item?

**Answer:**

| | |
|---|---|
| original amount = $1,500<br>percent change = 45% = 0.45<br>amount of change = ? | Identify the variables. |
| amount of change = original amount × percent change<br>= 1500 × 0.45 = 675 | Plug the variables into the appropriate equation. |
| 1500 − 675 = 825<br>**The final price is $825.** | To find the new price, subtract the amount of change from the original price. |

2) A house was bought in 2000 for $100,000 and sold in 2015 for $120,000. What was the percent growth in the value of the house from 2000 to 2015?

**Answer:**

| | |
|---|---|
| original amount = $100,000<br>amount of change = 120,000 − 100,000 = 20,000<br>percent change = ? | Identify the variables. |
| percent change = $\dfrac{\text{amount of change}}{\text{original amount}}$<br>= $\dfrac{20,000}{100,000}$<br>= 0.20 | Plug the variables into the appropriate equation. |
| 0.20 × 100 = **20%** | To find the percent growth, multiply by 100. |

# Comparison of Rational Numbers

Rational numbers can be ordered from least to greatest (or greatest to least) by placing them in the order in which they fall on a number line. When comparing a set of fractions, it's often easiest to convert each value to a common denominator. Then, it's only necessary to compare the numerators of each fraction.

When working with numbers in multiple forms (for example, a group of fractions and decimals), convert the values so that the set contains only fractions or only decimals. When ordering negative numbers, remember that the negative numbers with the largest absolute values are farthest from 0 and are therefore the smallest numbers. (For example, –75 is smaller than –25.)

Drawing a number line can help when comparing numbers: the final list should go in order from left to right (least to greatest) or right to left (greatest to least) on the line.

## EXAMPLES

1) Order the following numbers from greatest to least: $-\frac{2}{3}$, 1.2, 0, $-2.1$, $\frac{5}{4}$, $-1$, $\frac{1}{8}$.

   **Answer:**

   | | |
   |---|---|
   | $-\frac{2}{3} = -0.\overline{66}$ <br> $\frac{5}{4} = 1.25$ <br> $\frac{1}{8} = 0.125$ | Change each fraction to a decimal. |
   | $1.25, 1.2, 0.125, 0, -0.\overline{66}, -1,$ <br> $-2.1$ | Place the decimals in order from greatest to least. |
   | $\frac{5}{4}, 1.2, \frac{1}{8}, 0, -\frac{2}{3}, -1, -2.1$ | Convert back to fractions if the problem requires it. |

2) Order the following numbers from least to greatest: $\frac{1}{3}$, $-\frac{5}{6}$, $1\frac{1}{8}$, $\frac{7}{12}$, $-\frac{3}{4}$, $-\frac{3}{2}$.

   **Answer:**

   | | |
   |---|---|
   | $\frac{1}{3} = \frac{8}{24}$ <br><br> $-\frac{5}{6} = -\frac{20}{24}$ <br><br> $1\frac{1}{8} = \frac{9}{8} = \frac{27}{24}$ <br><br> $\frac{7}{12} = \frac{14}{24}$ <br><br> $-\frac{3}{4} = -\frac{18}{24}$ <br><br> $-\frac{3}{2} = -\frac{36}{24}$ | Convert each value using the least common denominator of 24. |
   | $-\frac{36}{24}, -\frac{20}{24}, -\frac{18}{24}, \frac{8}{24}, \frac{14}{24}, \frac{27}{24}$ | Arrange the fractions in order from least to greatest by comparing the numerators. |
   | $-\frac{3}{2}, -\frac{5}{6}, -\frac{3}{4}, \frac{1}{3}, \frac{7}{12}, 1\frac{1}{8}$ | Put the fractions back in their original form if the problem requires it. |

# Exponents and Radicals

## Exponents

An expression in the form $b^n$ is in an exponential notation where $b$ is the **BASE** and $n$ is an **EXPONENT**. To perform the operation, multiply the base by itself the number of times indicated by the exponent. For example, $2^3$ is equal to $2 \times 2 \times 2$ or 8.

Table 1.4. Operations with Exponents

| RULE | EXAMPLE | EXPLANATION |
|---|---|---|
| $a^0 = 1$ | $5^0 = 1$ | Any base (except 0) to the 0 power is 1. |
| $a^{-n} = \dfrac{1}{a^n}$ | $5^{-3} = \dfrac{1}{5^3}$ | A negative exponent becomes positive when moved from numerator to denominator (or vice versa). |
| $a^m a^n = a^{m+n}$ | $5^3 5^4 = 5^{3+4} = 5^7$ | Add the exponents to multiply two powers with the same base. |
| $(a^m)^n = a^{m \times n}$ | $(5^3)^4 = 5^{3(4)} = 5^{12}$ | Multiply the exponents to raise a power to a power. |
| $\dfrac{a^m}{a^n} = a^{m-n}$ | $\dfrac{5^4}{5^3} = 5^{4-3} = 5^1$ | Subtract the exponents to divide two powers with the same base. |
| $(ab)^n = a^n b^n$ | $(5 \times 6)^3 = 5^3 6^3$ | Apply the exponent to each base to raise a product to a power. |
| $\left(\dfrac{a}{b}\right)^n = \dfrac{a^n}{b^n}$ | $\left(\dfrac{5}{6}\right)^3 = \dfrac{5^3}{6^3}$ | Apply the exponent to each base to raise a quotient to a power. |
| $\left(\dfrac{a}{b}\right)^{-n} = \left(\dfrac{b}{a}\right)^n$ | $\left(\dfrac{5}{6}\right)^{-3} = \left(\dfrac{6}{5}\right)^3$ | Invert the fraction and change the sign of the exponent to raise a fraction to a negative power. |
| $\dfrac{a^m}{b^n} = \dfrac{b^{-n}}{a^{-m}}$ | $\dfrac{5^3}{6^4} = \dfrac{6^{-4}}{5^{-3}}$ | Change the sign of the exponent when moving a number from the numerator to denominator (or vice versa). |

## EXAMPLES

1) Simplify: $\dfrac{(10^2)^3}{(10^2)^2}$

**Answer:**

| $\dfrac{(10^2)^3}{(10^2)^2}$ | |
|---|---|
| $= \dfrac{10^6}{10^4}$ | Multiply the exponents raised to a power. |

| | |
|---|---|
| $= 10^{6-4}$ | Subtract the exponent in the denominator from the one in the numerator. |
| $= 10^2$ $= \mathbf{100}$ | Simplify. |

2) Simplify: $\dfrac{(x^{-2}y^2)^2}{x^3y}$

**Answer:**

| | |
|---|---|
| $\dfrac{(x^{-2}y^2)^2}{x^3y}$ | |
| $= \dfrac{x^{-4}y^4}{x^3y}$ | Multiply the exponents raised to a power. |
| $= x^{-4-3}y^{4-1}$ $= x^{-7}y^3$ | Subtract the exponent in the denominator from the one in the numerator. |
| $= \dfrac{y^3}{x^7}$ | Move negative exponents to the denominator. |

## Radicals

RADICALS are expressed as $\sqrt[b]{a}$, where $b$ is called the INDEX and $a$ is the RADICAND. A radical is used to indicate the inverse operation of an exponent: finding the base which can be raised to $b$ to yield $a$. For example, $\sqrt[3]{125}$ is equal to 5 because $5 \times 5 \times 5$ equals 125. The same operation can be expressed using a fraction exponent, so $\sqrt[b]{a} = a^{\frac{1}{b}}$. Note that when no value is indicated for $b$, it is assumed to be 2 (square root).

When $b$ is even and $a$ is positive, $\sqrt[b]{a}$ is defined to be the positive real value $n$ such that $n^b = a$ (example: $\sqrt{16} = 4$ only, and not $-4$, even though $(-4)(-4) = 16$). If $b$ is even and $a$ is negative, $\sqrt[b]{a}$ will be a complex number (example: $\sqrt{-9} = 3i$). Finally if $b$ is odd, $\sqrt[b]{a}$ will always be a real number regardless of the sign of $a$. If $a$ is negative, $\sqrt[b]{a}$ will be negative since a number to an odd power is negative (example: $\sqrt[5]{-32} = -2$ since $(-2)^5 = -32$).

$\sqrt[n]{x}$ is referred to as the $n$th root of $x$.

- $n = 2$ is the square root
- $n = 3$ is the cube root
- $n = 4$ is the fourth root
- $n = 5$ is the fifth root

The following table of operations with radicals holds for all cases EXCEPT the case where $b$ is even and $a$ is negative (the complex case).

Table 1.5. Operations with Radicals

| RULE | EXAMPLE | EXPLANATION |
|---|---|---|
| $\sqrt[b]{ac} = \sqrt[b]{a}\,\sqrt[b]{c}$ | $\sqrt[3]{81} = \sqrt[3]{27}\,\sqrt[3]{3} = 3\sqrt[3]{3}$ | The values under the radical sign can be separated into values that multiply to the original value. |
| $\sqrt[b]{\dfrac{a}{c}} = \dfrac{\sqrt[b]{a}}{\sqrt[b]{c}}$ | $\sqrt{\dfrac{4}{81}} = \dfrac{\sqrt{4}}{\sqrt{81}} = \dfrac{2}{9}$ | The $b$-root of the numerator and denominator can be calculated when there is a fraction under a radical sign. |
| $\sqrt[b]{a^c} = (\sqrt[b]{a})^c = a^{\frac{c}{b}}$ | $\sqrt[3]{6^2} = (\sqrt[3]{6})^2 = 6^{\frac{2}{3}}$ | The $b$-root can be written as a fractional exponent. If there is a power under the radical sign, it will be the numerator of the fraction. |
| $\dfrac{c}{\sqrt[b]{a}} \times \dfrac{\sqrt[b]{a}}{\sqrt[b]{a}} = \dfrac{c\sqrt[b]{a}}{a}$ | $\dfrac{5}{\sqrt{2}}\,\dfrac{\sqrt{2}}{\sqrt{2}} = \dfrac{5\sqrt{2}}{2}$ | To rationalize the denominator, multiply the numerator and denominator by the radical in the denominator until the radical has been canceled out. |
| $\dfrac{c}{b - \sqrt{a}} \times \dfrac{b + \sqrt{a}}{b + \sqrt{a}}$ $= \dfrac{c(b + \sqrt{a})}{b^2 - a}$ | $\dfrac{4}{3 - \sqrt{2}}\,\dfrac{3 + \sqrt{2}}{3 + \sqrt{2}}$ $= \dfrac{4(3 + \sqrt{2})}{9 - 2} = \dfrac{12 + 4\sqrt{2}}{7}$ | To rationalize the denominator, the numerator and denominator are multiplied by the conjugate of the denominator. |

## EXAMPLES

**1)** Simplify: $\sqrt{48}$

**Answer:**

| | |
|---|---|
| $\sqrt{48}$ | |
| $= \sqrt{16 \times 3}$ | Determine the largest square number that is a factor of the radicand (48) and write the radicand as a product using that square number as a factor. |
| $= \sqrt{16}\,\sqrt{3}$ $= \mathbf{4\sqrt{3}}$ | Apply the rules of radicals to simplify. |

**2)** Simplify: $\dfrac{6}{\sqrt{8}}$

**Answer:**

| | |
|---|---|
| $\dfrac{6}{\sqrt{8}}$ | |
| $= \dfrac{6}{\sqrt{4}\,\sqrt{2}}$ $= \dfrac{6}{2\sqrt{2}}$ | Apply the rules of radicals to simplify. |

$$= \frac{6}{2\sqrt{2}}\left(\frac{\sqrt{2}}{\sqrt{2}}\right)$$

$$= \frac{3\sqrt{2}}{2}$$

Multiply by $\frac{\sqrt{2}}{\sqrt{2}}$ to rationalize the denominator.

# Matrices

A **MATRIX** is a rectangular arrangement of numbers into **ROWS** (horizontal set of numbers) and **COLUMNS** (vertical set of numbers). A matrix with the same number of rows and columns is called a **SQUARE MATRIX**.

The **DIMENSIONS** of a matrix are given as $m \times n$, where $m$ is the number of rows and $n$ is the number of columns.

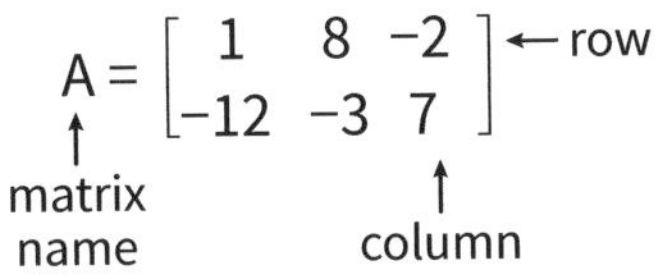

$$A = \begin{bmatrix} 1 & 8 & -2 \\ -12 & -3 & 7 \end{bmatrix} \leftarrow \text{row}$$

↑ matrix name    ↑ column

**Figure 1.3. Parts of a Matrix**

## Matrix Operations

Matrices can be added and subtracted together if and only if the matrices have the same dimensions. When the matrices have the same dimensions, the values in corresponding positions in the matrices can be added or subtracted. For example, the elements in row 1 column 1 from each matrix are added or subtracted. The matrix operation of addition is both commutative and associative: $A + B = B + A$ and $(A + B) + C = A + (B + C)$.

Matrices can be multiplied by a single value called a scalar. To perform this operation, each value in the matrix is multiplied by the scalar.

Two matrices can be multiplied only when the number of columns in the first matrix (with dimensions $m \times n$) equals the number of rows in the second matrix (dimensions $n \times p$). The resulting matrix will have dimensions $m \times p$. To complete the multiplication, the values in each row are multiplied by the corresponding values in each column (e.g., the first value in the row by the first value in the column, the second value in the row by the second value in the row, and so forth). The results of each row by column multiplication are then added together to give a single value. This resulting sum of products of row $a$ in the first matrix by column $b$ in the second matrix is placed in row $a$, column $b$ of the resulting matrix.

The matrix operation of multiplication is NOT commutative ($AB \neq BA$), but is associative ( $A(BC) = (AB)C$ ). The distributive property

$$\begin{bmatrix} a & b \\ c & d \end{bmatrix} \pm \begin{bmatrix} e & f \\ g & h \end{bmatrix} =$$

$$\begin{bmatrix} a \pm e & b \pm f \\ c \pm g & d \pm h \end{bmatrix} \times \begin{bmatrix} a & b \\ c & d \end{bmatrix} =$$

$$\begin{bmatrix} xa & xb \\ xc & xd \end{bmatrix}$$

of multiplication over addition also holds for matrices $(A(B + C) = AB + BC)$.

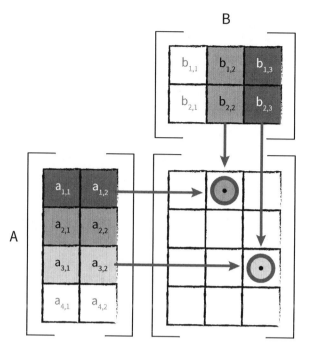

Figure 1.4. Matrix Multiplication

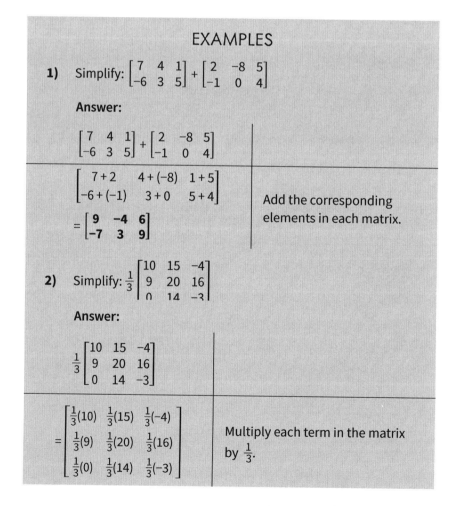

## EXAMPLES

1) Simplify: $\begin{bmatrix} 7 & 4 & 1 \\ -6 & 3 & 5 \end{bmatrix} + \begin{bmatrix} 2 & -8 & 5 \\ -1 & 0 & 4 \end{bmatrix}$

**Answer:**

| | |
|---|---|
| $\begin{bmatrix} 7 & 4 & 1 \\ -6 & 3 & 5 \end{bmatrix} + \begin{bmatrix} 2 & -8 & 5 \\ -1 & 0 & 4 \end{bmatrix}$ | |
| $\begin{bmatrix} 7+2 & 4+(-8) & 1+5 \\ -6+(-1) & 3+0 & 5+4 \end{bmatrix}$ $= \begin{bmatrix} 9 & -4 & 6 \\ -7 & 3 & 9 \end{bmatrix}$ | Add the corresponding elements in each matrix. |

2) Simplify: $\frac{1}{3}\begin{bmatrix} 10 & 15 & -4 \\ 9 & 20 & 16 \\ 0 & 14 & -3 \end{bmatrix}$

**Answer:**

| | |
|---|---|
| $\frac{1}{3}\begin{bmatrix} 10 & 15 & -4 \\ 9 & 20 & 16 \\ 0 & 14 & -3 \end{bmatrix}$ | |
| $= \begin{bmatrix} \frac{1}{3}(10) & \frac{1}{3}(15) & \frac{1}{3}(-4) \\ \frac{1}{3}(9) & \frac{1}{3}(20) & \frac{1}{3}(16) \\ \frac{1}{3}(0) & \frac{1}{3}(14) & \frac{1}{3}(-3) \end{bmatrix}$ | Multiply each term in the matrix by $\frac{1}{3}$. |

**3)** Simplify: $\begin{bmatrix} 1 & 0 & -2 \\ -3 & 4 & 1 \end{bmatrix} \begin{bmatrix} 3 & 0 \\ -2 & 4 \\ 1 & -4 \end{bmatrix}$

**Answer:**

$\begin{bmatrix} 1 & 0 & -2 \\ -3 & 4 & 1 \end{bmatrix} \begin{bmatrix} 3 & 0 \\ -2 & 4 \\ 1 & -4 \end{bmatrix}$

The matrices can be multiplied together because the number of columns in the first matrix equals the number of rows in the second matrix.

$= \begin{bmatrix} 1(3) + 0(-2) - 2(1) & 1(0) + 0(4) - 2(-4) \\ -3(3) + 4(-2) + 1(1) & -3(0) + 4(4) + 1(-4) \end{bmatrix}$

$= \begin{bmatrix} 3 + 0 - 2 & 0 + 0 + 8 \\ -9 - 8 + 1 & 0 + 16 - 4 \end{bmatrix}$

$= \begin{bmatrix} \mathbf{1} & \mathbf{8} \\ \mathbf{-16} & \mathbf{12} \end{bmatrix}$

Multiply the values in each row of the first matrix by the values in each column of the second and add. The resulting matrix is 2 × 2.

# Determinants

The **DETERMINANT** of a matrix (written as $\det(A)$ or $|A|$) is a value calculated by manipulating elements of a square matrix. The determinant of a 2 × 2 or a 3 × 3 matrix can easily be found by hand, but determinants of larger matrices are usually found using a calculator.

$$\begin{vmatrix} a & b \\ c & d \end{vmatrix} = ad - bc$$

$$\begin{vmatrix} a & b & c \\ d & e & f \\ g & h & i \end{vmatrix} = a \begin{vmatrix} e & f \\ h & i \end{vmatrix} - b \begin{vmatrix} d & f \\ g & i \end{vmatrix} + c \begin{vmatrix} d & e \\ g & h \end{vmatrix}$$

$$= a(ei - fh) - b(di - fg) + c(dh - eg)$$

## EXAMPLES

**1)** Find the determinant of the matrix $\begin{bmatrix} 7 & -3 \\ 4 & -2 \end{bmatrix}$.

**Answer:**

$\begin{vmatrix} 7 & -3 \\ 4 & -2 \end{vmatrix}$

$= 7(-2) - (-3)(4)$

$= -14 + 12$

$= \mathbf{-2}$

Use the formula to find the determinant of a 2 × 2 matrix.

**2)** Find the determinant of the matrix $\begin{bmatrix} -2 & 4 & 1 \\ 0 & 3 & -5 \\ 7 & -1 & 4 \end{bmatrix}$.

**Answer:**

$$\begin{bmatrix} -2 & 4 & 1 \\ 0 & 3 & -5 \\ 7 & -1 & 4 \end{bmatrix}$$

$$\begin{vmatrix} -2 & 4 & 1 \\ 0 & 3 & -5 \\ 7 & -1 & 4 \end{vmatrix}$$

$$= -2 \begin{vmatrix} 3 & -5 \\ -1 & 4 \end{vmatrix} - 4 \begin{vmatrix} 0 & -5 \\ 7 & 4 \end{vmatrix} + 1 \begin{vmatrix} 0 & 3 \\ 7 & -1 \end{vmatrix}$$

$$= -2(3(4) - (-5)(-1)) - 4(0(4) - (-5)7) + 1(0(-1) - 7(3))$$

$$= -2(12 - 5) - 4(0 + 35) + 1(0 - 21)$$

$$= -2(7) - 4(35) + 1(-21)$$

$$= -14 - 140 - 21$$

$$= \mathbf{-175}$$

Use the formula to find the determinant of a 3 × 3 matrix.

# Identity and Inverse Matrices

The **IDENTITY MATRIX** ($I$) is a square matrix with values of 1 forming a diagonal from the upper left corner to the bottom right corner; the rest of the elements are 0. When performing multiplication, the identity matrix functions like the number 1: the product of a matrix $A$ and the identity matrix $I$ returns the original matrix $A$ ($A \times I = A$).

$$\begin{bmatrix} 1 & 0 & 0 \\ 0 & 1 & 0 \\ 0 & 0 & 1 \end{bmatrix}$$

Figure 1.5. Identity Matrix

An **INVERSE MATRIX** ($A^{-1}$) is a square matrix that, when multiplied by the original matrix, results in the identity matrix ($A \times A^{-1} = I$). An inverse matrix can only be calculated for square matrices. A matrix is not invertible if its determinant is 0 (since the formula requires dividing by the determinant and division by 0 is not defined).

$$\begin{bmatrix} a & b \\ c & d \end{bmatrix}^{-1} = \frac{1}{ad - bc} \begin{bmatrix} d & -b \\ -c & a \end{bmatrix}$$

$$\begin{bmatrix} a & b & c \\ d & e & f \\ g & h & i \end{bmatrix}^{-1} = \frac{1}{\det A} \begin{bmatrix} ei - fh & ch - bi & bf - ce \\ fg - di & ai - cg & cd - af \\ dh - eg & bg - ah & ae - bd \end{bmatrix}$$

Multiplying a matrix by its inverse functions like division for matrices. (Note that there is no "real" division for matrices.) This operation can be used to solve matrix equations by setting up a system of equations using matrices (as discussed in "Matrix Operations").

## EXAMPLES

**1)** If $A = \begin{bmatrix} 2 & 3 \\ -1 & 4 \end{bmatrix}$, find $A^{-1}$.

**Answer:**

$\begin{bmatrix} 2 & 3 \\ -1 & 4 \end{bmatrix}^{-1}$

|  |  |
|---|---|
| $= \dfrac{1}{11}\begin{bmatrix} 4 & -3 \\ 1 & 2 \end{bmatrix}$ $= \begin{bmatrix} \dfrac{4}{11} & \dfrac{-3}{11} \\ \dfrac{1}{11} & \dfrac{2}{11} \end{bmatrix}$ | Use the formula to find the inverse of a 2 × 2 matrix. |

Check the answer: $A \times A^{-1} = \begin{bmatrix} 2 & 3 \\ -1 & 4 \end{bmatrix}\begin{bmatrix} \dfrac{4}{11} & \dfrac{-3}{11} \\ \dfrac{1}{11} & \dfrac{2}{11} \end{bmatrix} = \begin{bmatrix} 1 & 0 \\ 0 & 1 \end{bmatrix}$

**52)** Find the inverse matrix of $\begin{bmatrix} 1 & -1 & 2 \\ -1 & 0 & -2 \\ 2 & 1 & -2 \end{bmatrix}$.

**Answer:**

$\begin{bmatrix} 1 & -1 & 2 \\ -1 & 0 & -2 \\ 2 & 1 & -2 \end{bmatrix}^{-1}$

|  |  |
|---|---|
| $= \dfrac{1}{6}\begin{bmatrix} 0(-2)-(-2)1 & 2(1)-(-1)(-2) & (-1)(-2)-2(0) \\ (-2)(2)-(-1)(-2) & 1(-2)-2(2) & 2(-1)-1(-2) \\ (-1)(1)-0(2) & (-1)2-1(1) & 1(0)-(-1)(-1) \end{bmatrix}$ | Use the formula to find the inverse of a 3 × 3 matrix. |
| $= \dfrac{1}{6}\begin{bmatrix} 2 & 0 & 2 \\ -6 & -6 & 0 \\ -1 & -3 & -1 \end{bmatrix}$ $= \begin{bmatrix} \dfrac{1}{3} & 0 & \dfrac{1}{3} \\ -1 & -1 & 0 \\ -\dfrac{1}{6} & -\dfrac{1}{2} & -\dfrac{1}{6} \end{bmatrix}$ | Use the formula to find the inverse of a 3 × 3 matrix. |

# Factorials

A **FACTORIAL** of a number $n$ is denoted by $n!$ and is equal to $1 \times 2 \times 3 \times 4 \times ... \times n$. Both $0!$ and $1!$ are equal to 1 by definition. Fractions containing factorials can often be simplified by crossing out the portions of the factorials that occur in both the numerator and denominator.

## EXAMPLES

**29)** Simplify: 8!

**Answer:**

8!

| | |
|---|---|
| $= 8 \times 7 \times 6 \times 5 \times 4 \times 3 \times 2 \times 1$ <br> $= \textbf{40,320}$ | Expand the factorial and multiply. |

**30)** Simplify: $\dfrac{10!}{7!3!}$

**Answer:**

$\dfrac{10!}{7!3!}$

| | |
|---|---|
| $= \dfrac{10 \times 9 \times 8 \times 7!}{7! \times 3 \times 2 \times 1}$ | Expand the factorial. |
| $= \dfrac{10 \times 9 \times 8}{3 \times 2 \times 1}$ | Cross out values that occur in both the numerator and denominator. |
| $= \dfrac{720}{6}$ <br> $= \textbf{120}$ | Multiply and simplify. |

# Sequences and Series

Sequences can be thought of as a set of numbers (called **TERMS**) with a rule that explains the particular pattern between the terms. The terms of a sequence are separated by commas. There are two types of sequences that will be examined, arithmetic and geometric. The sum of an arithmetic sequence is known as an **ARITHMETIC SERIES**; similarly the sum of a geometric sequence is known as a **GEOMETRIC SERIES**.

## Arithmetic Sequences

**ARITHMETIC GROWTH** is constant growth, meaning that the difference between any one term in the series and the next consecutive term will be the same constant. This constant is called the **COMMON DIFFERENCE**. Thus, to list the terms in the sequence, one can just add (or subtract) the same number repeatedly. For example, the series {20, 30, 40, 50} is arithmetic since 10 is added each time to get from one term to the next. One way to represent this sequence is using a **RECURSIVE** definition, which basically says: *next term = current term + common difference*. For this example, the recursive definition would be $a_{n+1} = a_n + 10$ because the *next* term $a_{n+1}$ in the sequence is the current term $a_n$ plus 10. In general, the recursive definition of a series is:

$a_{n+1} = a_n + d$, where $d$ is the common difference.

Often, the objective of arithmetic sequence questions is to find a specific term in the sequence or the sum of a certain series of terms. The formulas to use are:

Table 1.6. Formulas for Arithmetic Sequences and Series

### FINDING THE *N*TH TERM . . .

| | |
|---|---|
| $a_n = a_1 + d(n-1)$ $a_n = a_m + d(n-m)$ | $d$ = the common difference of the sequence $a_n$ = the *n*th term in the sequence $n$ = the number of the term $a_m$ = the *m*th term in the sequence $m$ = the number of the term $a_1$ = the first term in the sequence |

### FINDING THE PARTIAL SUM . . .

| | |
|---|---|
| $S_n = \dfrac{n(a_1 + a_n)}{2}$ | $S_n$ = sum of the terms through the *n*th term $a_n$ = the *n*th term in the sequence $n$ = the number of the term $a_1$ = the first term in the sequence |

## EXAMPLES

1) Find the ninth term of the sequence: −57, −40, −23, −6 …

**Answer:**

| | |
|---|---|
| $a_1 = -57$ $d = -57 - (-40) = 17$ $n = 9$ | Identify the variables given. |
| $a_9 = -57 + 17(9 - 1)$ | Plug these values into the formula for the specific term of an arithmetic sequence. |
| $a_9 = -57 + 17(8)$ $a_9 = -57 + 136$ $\boldsymbol{a_9 = 79}$ | Solve for $a_9$. |

2) If the 23rd term in an arithmetic sequence is 820, and the 5th term is 200, find the common difference between each term.

**Answer:**

| | |
|---|---|
| $a_5 = 200$ $a_{23} = 820$ $n = 23$ $m = 5$ $d = ?$ | Idenfity the variables given. |

| | |
|---|---|
| $a_n = a_m + d(n-m)$ <br> $820 = 200 + d(23-5)$ <br> $620 = d(18)$ <br> **$d = 34.\overline{44}$** | Plug these values into the equation for using one term to find another in an arithmetic sequence. |

3) Evaluate $\sum_{n=14}^{45} 2n + 10$.

**Answer:**

| | |
|---|---|
| $a_1 = 2(1) + 10 = 12$ <br> $n = 45$ <br> $a_n = 2(45) + 10 = 100$ <br> $S_n = \dfrac{n(a_1 + a_n)}{2}$ <br> $= \dfrac{45(12 + 100)}{2}$ <br> $= 2520$ | Find the partial sum of the first 45 terms. |
| $a_1 = 2(1) + 10 = 12$ <br> $n = 13$ <br> $a_n = 2(13) + 10 = 36$ <br> $S_n = \dfrac{n(a_1 + a_n)}{2}$ <br> $= \dfrac{13(12 + 36)}{2}$ <br> $= 312$ | Find the partial sum of the first 13 terms. |
| $S_{45} - S_{13} = 2520 - 312$ <br> **$= 2208$** | The sum of the terms between 14 and 45 will be the difference between $S_{45}$ and $S_{13}$. |

# Geometric Sequences

While an arithmetic sequence has an additive pattern, a GEOMETRIC SEQUENCE has a multiplicative pattern. This means that to get from any one term in the sequence to the next term in the sequence, the term is multiplied by a fixed number (called the COMMON RATIO). The following sequence is a geometric sequence: {8, 4, 2, 1, .5, .25, .125}. In this case, the multiplier (or common ratio) is $\frac{1}{2}$. The multiplier can be any real number other than 0 or 1. To find the common ratio, simply choose any term in the sequence and divide it by the previous term (this is the ratio of two consecutive terms—thus the name common *ratio*). In the above example, the ratio between the second and third terms is $\frac{2}{4} = \frac{1}{2}$.

Geometric sequences require their own formulas to find the next term and a sum of a specific series.

Table 1.7. Geometric Sequences: Formulas

### FINDING THE *N*TH TERM . . .

$$a_n = a_1 \times r^{n-1}$$
$$a_n = a_m \times r^{n-m}$$

$r$ = the common ratio of the sequence
$a_n$ = the $n$th term in the sequence
$n$ = the number of the term
$a_m$ = the $m$th term in the sequence
$m$ = the number of the term
$a_1$ = the first term in the sequence

### FINDING THE PARTIAL SUM . . .

$$S_n = \frac{a_1(1 - r^n)}{1 - r}$$

$S_n$ = sum of the terms through the $n$th term
$r$ = the common ratio of the sequence
$a_n$ = the $n$th term in the sequence
$n$ = the number of the term
$a_1$ = the first term in the sequence

### FINDING THE SUM OF AN INFINITE SERIES . . .

$$S_\infty = \frac{a}{1 - r}$$
$$(|r| < 1)$$

$S_\infty$ = sum of all terms
$r$ = the common ratio of the sequence
$a$ = the fifth term in the sequence

The finite sum formula works similarly to the arithmetic sequence sum. However, sometimes the INFINITE SUM of the sequence must be found. The sum of an infinite number of terms of a sequence is called a SERIES. If the infinite terms of the sequence add up to a finite number, the series is said to CONVERGE to that number. If the sum of the terms is infinite, then the series DIVERGES. Another way to say this is to ask: is there a limit to the finite sum $S_n$ as $n$ goes to infinity? For geometric series in the form $\sum_{n=1}^{\infty} a \times r^n$, the series converges only when $|r| < 1$ (or $-1 < r < 1$). If $r$ is greater than 1, the sum will approach infinity, so the series diverges.

Compared to arithmetic growth, geometric growth is much faster. As seen in the formulas used to find a geometric term, geometric growth is exponential, whereas arithmetic growth is linear.

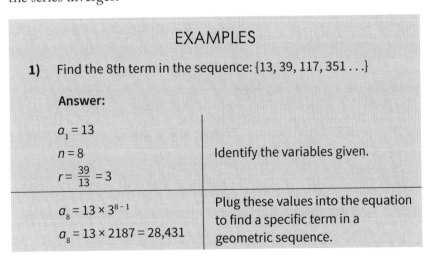

## EXAMPLES

1) Find the 8th term in the sequence: {13, 39, 117, 351 . . .}

**Answer:**

| | |
|---|---|
| $a_1 = 13$ $n = 8$ $r = \frac{39}{13} = 3$ | Identify the variables given. |
| $a_8 = 13 \times 3^{8-1}$ $a_8 = 13 \times 2187 = 28{,}431$ | Plug these values into the equation to find a specific term in a geometric sequence. |

The eighth term of
the given sequence is
**28,431**.

2) Find the sum of the first 10 terms of this sequence: $\{-4, 16, -64, 256\ldots\}$

**Answer:**

| | |
|---|---|
| $a_1 = -4$ <br> $n = 10$ <br> $r = \frac{16}{-4} = -4$ | Identify the variables given. |
| $S_{10} = \frac{-4(1-(-4)^{10})}{1-(-4)}$ <br><br> $= \frac{-4(1-1,048,576)}{5}$ <br><br> $= \frac{4,194,300}{5}$ <br><br> $= \textbf{838,860}$ | Plug these values into the equation for the partial sum of a geometric sequence. |

# two

# ALGEBRA AND FUCTIONS

Algebra, meaning "restoration" in Arabic, is the mathematical method of finding the unknown. The first algebraic book in Egypt was used to figure out complex inheritances that were to be split among many individuals. Today, algebra is just as necessary when dealing with unknown amounts.

## Algebraic Expressions

The foundation of algebra is the **VARIABLE**, an unknown number represented by a symbol (usually a letter such as $x$ or $a$). Variables can be preceded by a **COEFFICIENT**, which is a constant (i.e., a real number) in front of the variable, such as $4x$ or $-2a$. An **ALGEBRAIC EXPRESSION** is any sum, difference, product, or quotient of variables and numbers (for example $3x^2$, $2x + 7y - 1$, and $\frac{5}{x}$ are algebraic expressions). **TERMS** are any quantities that are added or subtracted (for example, the terms of the expression $x^2 - 3x + 5$ are $x^2$, $3x$, and 5). A **POLYNOMIAL EXPRESSION** is an algebraic expression where all the exponents on the variables are whole numbers. A polynomial with only two terms is known as a **BINOMIAL**, and one with three terms is a **TRINOMIAL**. A **MONOMIAL** has only one term.

**EVALUATING EXPRESSIONS** is another way of saying "find the numeric value of an expression if the variable is equal to a certain number." To evaluate the expression, simply plug the given value(s) for the variable(s) into the equation and simplify. Remember to use the order of operations when simplifying:

1. Parentheses
2. Exponents
3. Multiplication
4. Division
5. Addition
6. Subtraction

Simplified expressions are ordered by variable terms alphabetically with highest exponent first then down to constants.

# Operations with Expressions

## Adding and Subtracting

Expressions can be added or subtracted by simply adding and subtracting LIKE TERMS, which are terms with the same variable part (the variables must be the same, with the same exponents on each variable). For example, in the expressions $2x + 3xy - 2z$ and $6y + 2xy$, the like terms are $3xy$ and $2xy$. Adding the two expressions yields the new expression $2x + 6xy - 2z + 6y$. Note that the other terms did not change; they cannot be combined because they have different variables.

## Distributing and Factoring

Distributing and factoring can be seen as two sides of the same coin. DISTRIBUTION multiplies each term in the first factor by each term in the second factor to get rid of parentheses. FACTORING reverses this process, taking a polynomial in standard form and writing it as a product of two or more factors.

Operations with polynomials can always be checked by evaluating equivalent expressions for the same value.

When distributing a monomial through a polynomial, the expression outside the parentheses is multiplied by each term inside the parentheses. Using the rules of exponents, coefficients are multiplied and exponents are added.

When simplifying two polynomials, each term in the first polynomial must multiply each term in the second polynomial. A binomial (two terms) multiplied by a binomial, will require 2 × 2 or 4 multiplications. For the binomial × binomial case, this process is sometimes called **FOIL**, which stands for first, outside, inside, and last. These terms refer to the placement of each term of the expression: multiply the first term in each expression, then the outside terms, then the inside terms, and finally the last terms. A binomial (two terms) multiplied by a trinomial (three terms), will require 2 × 3 or 6 products to simplify. The first term in the first polynomial multiplies each of the three terms in the second polynomial, then the second term in the first polynomial multiplies each of the three terms in the second polynomial. A trinomial (three terms) by a trinomial will require 3 × 3 or 9 products, and so on.

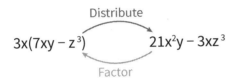

**Figure 2.1. Distribution and Factoring**

Factoring is the reverse of distributing: the first step is always to remove ("undistribute") the GCF of all the terms, if there is a GCF (besides 1). The GCF is the product of any constants and/or variables that <u>every</u> term shares. (For example, the GCF of $12x^3$, $15x^2$ and $6xy^2$ is $3x$ because $3x$ evenly divides all three terms.) This shared factor can be taken out of each term and moved to the outside of the parentheses, leaving behind a polynomial where each term is the original term divided by the GCF. (The remaining terms for the terms in the example would be $4x^2$, $5x$, and $2xy$.) It may be possible to factor the polynomial in the parentheses further, depending on the problem.

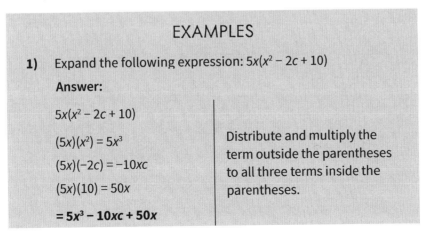

EXAMPLES

1) Expand the following expression: $5x(x^2 - 2c + 10)$

**Answer:**

$5x(x^2 - 2c + 10)$

$(5x)(x^2) = 5x^3$

$(5x)(-2c) = -10xc$

$(5x)(10) = 50x$

Distribute and multiply the term outside the parentheses to all three terms inside the parentheses.

$= 5x^3 - 10xc + 50x$

**2)** Expand the following expression: $(x^2 - 5)(2x - x^3)$

**Answer:**

| | |
|---|---|
| $(x^2 - 5)(2x - x^3)$ <br> $(x^2)(2x) = 2x^3$ <br> $(x^2)(-x^3) = -x^5$ <br> $(-5)(2x) = -10x$ <br> $(-5)(-x^3) = 5x^3$ | Apply FOIL: first, outside, inside, and last. |
| $= 2x^3 - x^5 - 10x + 5x^3$ | Combine like terms and put them in order. |
| $= -x^5 + 7x^3 - 10x$ | |

**3)** Factor the expression $16z^2 + 48z$

**Answer:**

| | |
|---|---|
| $16z^2 + 48z$ <br> $= 16z(z + 3)$ | Both terms have a $z$, and 16 is a common factor of both 16 and 48. So the greatest common factor is $16z$. Factor out the GCF. |

**4)** Factor the expression $6m^3 + 12m^3n - 9m^2$

**Answer:**

| | |
|---|---|
| $6m^3 + 12m^3n - 9m^2$ <br> $= 3m^2(2m + 4mn - 3)$ | All the terms share the factor $m^2$, and 3 is the greatest common factor of 6, 12, and 9. So, the GCF is $3m^2$. |

## Factoring Trinomials

If the leading coefficient is $a = 1$, the trinomial is in the form $x^2 + bx + c$ and can often be rewritten in the factored form, as a product of two binomials: $(x + m)(x + n)$. Recall that the product of two binomials can be written in expanded form $x^2 + mx + nx + mn$. Equating this expression with $x^2 + bx + c$, the constant term $c$ would have to equal the product $mn$. Thus, to work backward from the trinomial to the factored form, consider all the numbers $m$ and $n$ that multiply to make $c$. For example, to factor $x^2 + 8x + 12$, consider all the pairs that multiply to be 12 ($12 = 1 \times 12$ or $2 \times 6$ or $3 \times 4$). Choose the pair that will make the coefficient of the middle term (8) when added. In this example 2 and 6 add to 8, so making $m = 2$ and $n = 6$ in the expanded form gives:

| | |
|---|---|
| $x^2 + 8x + 12 = x^2 + 2x + 6x + 12$ | |
| $= (x^2 + 2x) + (6x + 12)$ | Group the first two terms and the last two terms. |
| $= x(x + 6) + 2(x + 6)$ | Factor the GCF out of each set of parentheses. |

$$= (x + 6)(x + 2)$$

The two terms now have the common factor $(x + 6)$, which can be removed, leaving $(x + 2)$ and the original polynomial is factored.

In general:

$x^2 + bx + c = x^2 + mx + nx + mn$, where $c = mn$ and $b = m + n$

| | |
|---|---|
| $= (x^2 + mx) + (nx + mn)$ | Group. |
| $= x(x + m) + n(x + m)$ | Factor each group. |
| $= (x + m)(x + n)$ | Factor out the common binomial. |

Note that if none of the factors of $c$ add to the value $b$, then the trinomial cannot be factored, and is called PRIME.

If the leading coefficient is not 1 ($a \neq 1$), first make sure that any common factors among the three terms are factored out. If the $a$-value is negative, factor out –1 first as well. If the $a$-value of the new polynomial in the parentheses is still not 1, follow this rule: Identify two values $r$ and $s$ that multiply to be $ac$ and add to be $b$. Then write the polynomial in this form: $ax^2 + bx + c = ax^2 + rx + sx + c$, and proceed by grouping, factoring, and removing the common binomial as above.

There are a few special factoring cases worth memorizing: difference of squares, binomial squared, and the sum and difference of cubes.

- **DIFFERENCE OF SQUARES** (each term is a square and they are subtracted):
  - $a^2 - b^2 = (a + b)(a - b)$
  - Note that a SUM of squares is never factorable.
- **BINOMIAL SQUARED:**
  - $a^2 + 2ab + b^2 = (a + b)(a + b) = (a + b)^2$
- **SUM AND DIFFERENCE OF CUBES:**
  - $a^3 + b^3 = (a + b)(a^2 - ab + b^2)$
  - $a^3 - b^3 = (a - b)(a^2 + ab + b^2)$
  - Note that the second factor in these factorizations will never be able to be factored further.

## EXAMPLES

**1)** Factor: $16x^2 + 52x + 30$

**Answer:**

| | |
|---|---|
| $16x^2 + 52x + 30$ | |
| $= 2(8x^2 + 26x + 15)$ | Remove the GCF of 2. |

| | |
|---|---|
| $= 2(8x^2 + 6x + 20x + 15)$ | To factor the polynomial in the parentheses, calculate $ac = (8)(15) = 120$, and consider all the pairs of numbers that multiply to be 120: $1 \times 120$, $2 \times 60$, $3 \times 40$, $4 \times 30$, $5 \times 24$, $6 \times 20$, $8 \times 15$, and $10 \times 12$. Of these pairs, choose the pair that adds to be the $b$-value 26 (6 and 20). |
| $= 2[(8x^2 + 6x) + (20x + 15)]$ | Group. |
| $= 2[2x(4x + 3) + 5(4x + 3)]$ | Factor out the GCF of each group. |
| $= 2[(4x + 3)(2x + 5)]$ | Factor out the common binomial. |
| $\mathbf{2(4x + 3)(2x + 5)}$ | |

If there are no values $r$ and $s$ that multiply to be $ac$ and add to be $b$, then the polynomial is prime and cannot be factored.

**2)** Factor: $-21x^2 - x + 10$

**Answer:**

| | |
|---|---|
| $-21x^2 - x + 10$ | |
| $= -(21x^2 + x - 10)$ | Factor out the negative. |
| $= -(21x^2 - 14x + 15x - 10)$ | Factor the polynomial in the parentheses.<br><br>$ac = 210$ and $b = 1$<br><br>The numbers 15 and −14 can be multiplied to get 210 and subtracted to get 1. |
| $= -[(21x^2 - 14x) + (15x - 10)]$ | Group. |
| $= -[7x(3x - 2) + 5(3x - 2)]$ | Factor out the GCF of each group. |
| $\mathbf{= -(3x - 2)(7x + 5)}$ | Factor out the common binomial. |

# Linear Equations

An EQUATION states that two expressions are equal to each other. Polynomial equations are categorized by the highest power of the variables they contain: the highest power of any exponent of a linear equation is 1, a quadratic equation has a variable raised to the second power, a cubic equation has a variable raised to the third power, and so on.

## Solving Linear Equations

Solving an equation means finding the value or values of the variable that make the equation true. To solve a linear equation, it is necessary to manipulate the terms so that the variable being solved for appears alone on one side of the equal sign while everything else in the equation is on the other side.

The way to solve linear equations is to "undo" all the operations that connect numbers to the variable of interest. Follow these steps:

1. Eliminate fractions by multiplying each side by the least common multiple of any denominators.

2. Distribute to eliminate parentheses, braces, and brackets.

3. Combine like terms.

4. Use addition or subtraction to collect all terms containing the variable of interest to one side, and all terms not containing the variable to the other side.

5. Use multiplication or division to remove coefficients from the variable of interest.

Sometimes there are no numeric values in the equation or there are a mix of numerous variables and constants. The goal is to solve the equation for one of the variables in terms of the other variables. In this case, the answer will be an expression involving numbers and letters instead of a numeric value.

On multiple choice tests, it is often easier to plug the possible values into the equation and determine which solution makes the equation true than to solve the equation.

## EXAMPLES

**1)** Solve for $x$: $\dfrac{100(x+5)}{20} = 1$

**Answer:**

| | |
|---|---|
| $\dfrac{100(x+5)}{20} = 1$ | |
| $(20)\left(\dfrac{100(x+5)}{20}\right) = (1)(20)$ $100(x+5) = 20$ | Multiply both sides by 20 to cancel out the denominator. |
| $100x + 500 = 20$ | Distribute 100 through the parentheses. |
| $100x = -480$ | "Undo" the +500 by subtracting 500 on both sides of the equation to isolate the variable term. |
| $x = \dfrac{-480}{100}$ | "Undo" the multiplication by 100 by dividing by 100 on both sides to solve for $x$. |
| $x = -4.8$ | |

**2)** Solve for $x$: $2(x+2)^2 - 2x^2 + 10 = 42$

**Answer:**

| | |
|---|---|
| $2(x+2)^2 - 2x^2 + 10 = 42$ | |
| $2(x+2)(x+2) - 2x^2 + 10 = 42$ | Eliminate the exponents on the left side. |

| | |
|---|---|
| $2(x^2 + 4x + 4) - 2x^2 + 10 = 42$ | Apply FOIL. |
| $2x^2 + 8x + 8 - 2x^2 + 10 = 42$ | Distribute the 2. |
| $8x + 18 = 42$ | Combine like terms on the left-hand side. |
| $8x = 24$ | Isolate the variable. "Undo" +18 by subtracting 18 on both sides. |
| $x = 3$ | "Undo" multiplication by 8 by dividing both sides by 8. |

**3)** Solve the equation for $D$: $\dfrac{A(3B + 2D)}{2N} = 5M - 6$

**Answer:**

| | |
|---|---|
| $\dfrac{A(3B + 2D)}{2N} = 5M - 6$ | |
| $3AB + 2AD = 10MN - 12N$ | Multiply both sides by $2N$ to clear the fraction, and distribute the $A$ through the parentheses. |
| $2AD = 10MN - 12N - 3AB$ | Isolate the term with the $D$ in it by moving $3AB$ to the other side of the equation. |
| $D = \dfrac{(10MN - 12N - 3AB)}{2A}$ | Divide both sides by $2A$ to get $D$ alone on the right-hand side. |

# Graphs of Linear Equations

The most common way to write a linear equation is SLOPE-INTERCEPT FORM, $y = mx + b$. In this equation, $m$ is the slope, which describes how steep the line is, and $b$ is the $y$-intercept. Slope is often described as "rise over run" because it is calculated as the difference in $y$-values (rise) over the difference in $x$-values (run). The slope of the line is also the rate of change of the dependent variable $y$ with respect to the independent variable $x$. The $y$-intercept is the point where the line crosses the $y$-axis, or where $x$ equals zero.

To graph a linear equation, identify the $y$-intercept and place that point on the $y$-axis. If the slope is not written as a fraction, make it a fraction by writing it over 1 $\left(\frac{m}{1}\right)$. Then use the slope to count up (or down, if negative) the "rise" part of the slope and over the "run" part of the slope to find a second point. These points can then be connected to draw the line.

To find the equation of a line, identify the $y$-intercept, if possible, on the graph and use two easily identifiable points to find the slope. If the $y$-intercept is not easily identified, identify the slope by choosing easily identifiable points; then choose one point on the graph, plug the point and the slope values into the equation, and solve for the missing value $b$.

Use the phrase "Begin, Move" to remember that b is the y-intercept (where to begin) and m is the slope (how the line moves).

slope-intercept form:
$y = mx + b$
slope:
$m = \dfrac{y_2 - y_1}{x_2 - x_1}$

- standard form: $Ax + By = C$
- $m = -\dfrac{A}{B}$
- $x$-intercept $= \dfrac{C}{A}$
- $y$-intercept $= \dfrac{C}{B}$

Another way to express a linear equation is standard form: $Ax + By = C$. In order to graph equations in this form, it is often easiest to convert them to point-slope form. Alternately, it is easy to find the $x$- or $y$-intercept from this form, and once these two points are known, a line can be drawn through them. To find the $x$-intercept, simply make $y = 0$ and solve for $x$. Similarly, to find the $y$-intercept, make $x = 0$ and solve for $y$.

## EXAMPLES

**1)** What is the slope of the line whose equation is $6x - 2y - 8 = 0$?

**Answer:**

| | |
|---|---|
| $6x - 2y - 8 = 0$ | |
| $-2y = -6x + 8$ <br> $y = \dfrac{-6x + 8}{-2}$ <br> $y = 3x - 4$ | Rearrange the equation into slope-intercept form by solving the equation for $y$. |
| $m = 3$ | The slope is 3, the value attached to $x$. |

**2)** What is the equation of the following line?

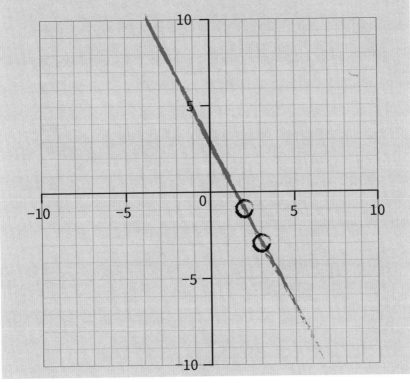

**Answer:**

| | |
|---|---|
| $b = 3$ | The $y$-intercept can be identified on the graph as $(0, 3)$. |
| $m = \frac{(-3) - (-1)}{3 - 2} = \frac{-2}{1} = -2$ | To find the slope, choose any two points and plug the values into the slope equation. The two points chosen here are $(2, -1)$ and $(3, -3)$. |
| $y = -2x + 3$ | Replace $m$ with $-2$ and $b$ with 3 in $y = mx + b$. |

3) Write the equation of the line which passes through the points $(-2, 5)$ and $(-5, 3)$.

**Answer:**

| | |
|---|---|
| $(-2, 5)$ and $(-5, 3)$ | |
| $m = \frac{3 - 5}{(-5) - (-2)}$ $= \frac{-2}{-3}$ $= \frac{2}{3}$ | Calculate the slope. |
| $5 = \frac{2}{3}(-2) + b$ $5 = \frac{-4}{3} + b$ $b = \frac{19}{3}$ | To find $b$, plug into the equation $y = mx + b$ the slope for $m$ and a set of points for $x$ and $y$. |
| $y = \frac{2}{3}x + \frac{19}{3}$ | Replace $m$ and $b$ to find the equation of the line. |

4) What is the equation of the following graph?

**Answer:**

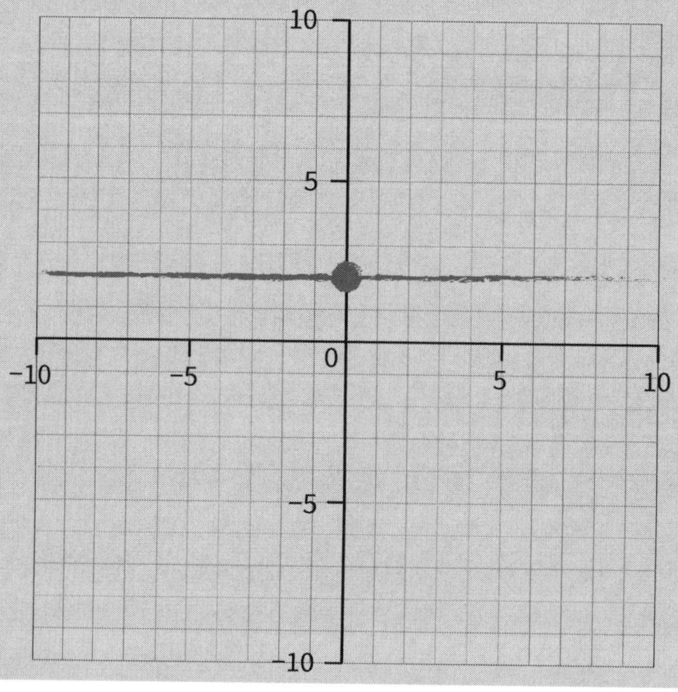

| | |
|---|---|
| $y = 0x + 2$, or $y = 2$ | The line has a rise of 0 and a run of 1, so the slope is $\frac{0}{1} = 0$. There is no $x$-intercept. The $y$-intercept is $(0, 2)$, meaning that the $b$-value in the slope-intercept form is 2. |

## Systems of Linear Equations

Systems of equations are sets of equations that include two or more variables. These systems can only be solved when there are at least as many equations as there are variables. Systems involve working with more than one equation to solve for more than one variable. For a system of linear equations, the solution to the system is the set of values for the variables that satisfies every equation in the system. Graphically, this will be the point where every line meets. If the lines are parallel (and hence do not intersect), the system will have no solution. If the lines are multiples of each other, meaning they share all coordinates, then the system has infinitely many solutions (because every point on the line is a solution).

Plug answers back into both equations to ensure the system has been solved properly.

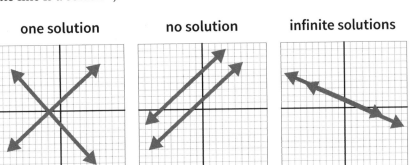

one solution          no solution          infinite solutions

Figure 2.2. Systems of Equations

There are three common methods for solving systems of equations. To perform SUBSTITUTION, solve one equation for one variable, and then plug in the resulting expression for that variable in the second equation. This process works best for systems of two equations with two variables where the coefficient of one or more of the variables is 1.

To solve using ELIMINATION, add or subtract two equations so that one or more variables are eliminated. It's often necessary to multiply one or both of the equations by a scalar (constant) in order to make the variables cancel. Equations can be added or subtracted as many times as necessary to find each variable.

Yet another way to solve a system of linear equations is to use a MATRIX EQUATION. In the matrix equation $AX = B$, $A$ contains the system's coefficients, $X$ contains the variables, and $B$ contains the constants (as shown below). The matrix equation can then be solved by multiplying $B$ by the inverse of $A$: $X = A^{-1}B$

$$ax + by = e$$
$$cx + dy = f$$
$$\rightarrow A = \begin{bmatrix} a & b \\ c & d \end{bmatrix} \quad X = \begin{bmatrix} x \\ y \end{bmatrix} \quad B = \begin{bmatrix} e \\ f \end{bmatrix} \quad \rightarrow AX = B$$

This method can be extended to equations with three or more variables. Technology (such as a graphing calculator) is often employed when solving using this method if more than two variables are involved.

## EXAMPLES

**1)** Solve for $x$ and $y$:

$2x - 4y = 28$

$4x - 12y = 36$

**Answer:**

| | |
|---|---|
| $2x - 4y = 28$ <br> $x = 2y + 14$ | Solve the system with substitution. Solve one equation for one variable. |
| $4x - 12y = 36$ <br> $4(2y + 14) - 12y = 36$ <br> $8y + 56 - 12y = 36$ <br> $-4y = -20$ <br> $y = 5$ | Plug in the resulting expression for $x$ in the second equation and simplify. |
| $2x - 4y = 28$ <br> $2x - 4(5) = 28$ <br> $2x - 20 = 28$ <br> $2x = 48$ <br> $x = 24$ <br> The answer is $y = 5$ and $x = 24$ or **(24, 5)**. | Plug the solved variable into either equation to find the second variable. |

**2)** Solve for the system for $x$ and $y$:

$3 = -4x + y$

$16x = 4y + 2$

**Answer:**

| | |
|---|---|
| $3 = -4x + y$ <br> $y = 4x + 3$ | Isolate the variable in one equation. |
| $16x = 4y + 2$ <br> $16x = 4(4x + 3) + 2$ <br> $16x = 16x + 12 + 2$ <br> $0 = 14$ <br> **No solution exists.** | Plug the expression into the second equation. <br><br> Both equations have slope 4. This means the graphs of the equations are parallel lines, so no intersection (solution) exists. |

**3)** Solve the system of equations:

$6x + 10y = 18$

$4x + 15y = 37$

**Answer:**

Because solving for $x$ or $y$ in either equation will result in messy fractions, this problem is best solved using elimination. The goal is to eliminate one of the variables by making the coefficients in front of one set of variables the same, but with different signs, and then adding both equations.

| | |
|---|---|
| $6x + 10y = 18 \xrightarrow[(-2)]{} {}^{-12}x\,{}^{-20}y = {}^{-36}$ <br> $4x + 15y = 37 \xrightarrow[(3)]{} {}^{12}x\,{}^{+45}y = {}^{1}\underline{11}$ | To eliminate the $x$'s in this problem, find the least common multiple of coefficients 6 and 4. The smallest number that both 6 and 4 divide into evenly is 12. Multiply the top equation by $-2$, and the bottom equation by 3. |
| $25y = 75$ | Add the two equations to eliminate the $x$'s. |
| $y = 3$ | Solve for $y$. |
| $6x + 10(3) = 18$ <br> $6x + 30 = 18$ <br> $x = -2$ | Replace $y$ with 3 in either of the original equations. |
| The solution is **(−2, 3).** | |

**4)** Solve the following systems of equations using matrix arithmetic:

$2x - 3y = -5$

$3x - 4y = -8$

**Answer:**

| | |
|---|---|
| $\begin{bmatrix} 2 & -3 \\ 3 & -4 \end{bmatrix} \begin{bmatrix} x \\ y \end{bmatrix} = \begin{bmatrix} -5 \\ -8 \end{bmatrix}$ | Write the system in matrix form, **$AX = B$**. |
| $\begin{bmatrix} 2 & -3 \\ 3 & -4 \end{bmatrix}^{-1}$ <br> $= \dfrac{1}{(2)(-4)-(-3)(3)} \begin{bmatrix} -4 & 3 \\ -3 & 2 \end{bmatrix} =$ <br> $\begin{bmatrix} -4 & 3 \\ -3 & 2 \end{bmatrix}$ | Calculate the inverse of Matrix **$A$**. |
| $\begin{bmatrix} x \\ y \end{bmatrix} = \begin{bmatrix} -4 & 3 \\ -3 & 2 \end{bmatrix} \begin{bmatrix} -5 \\ -8 \end{bmatrix} = \begin{bmatrix} -4 \\ -1 \end{bmatrix}$ | Multiply **$B$** by the inverse of **$A$**. |
| $x = -4$ <br> $y = -1$ | Match up the 2 × 1 matrices to identify $x$ and $y$. |

# Building Equations

In word problems, it is often necessary to translate a verbal description of a relationship into a mathematical equation. No matter the problem, this process can be done using the same steps:

1. Read the problem carefully and identify what value needs to be solved for.
2. Identify the known and unknown quantities in the problem, and assign the unknown quantities a variable.
3. Create equations using the variables and known quantities.
4. Solve the equations.
5. Check the solution: Does it answer the question asked in the problem? Does it make sense?

## EXAMPLES

1) A school is holding a raffle to raise money. There is a $3 entry fee, and each ticket costs $5. If a student paid $28, how many tickets did he buy?

**Answer:**

| | |
|---|---|
| Number of tickets = $x$<br>Cost per ticket = 5<br>Cost for $x$ tickets = $5x$<br>Total cost = 28<br>Entry fee = 3 | Identify the quantities. |
| $5x + 3 = 28$ | Set up equations. The total cost for $x$ tickets will be equal to the cost for $x$ tickets plus the $3 flat fee. |
| $5x + 3 = 28$<br>$5x = 25$<br>$x = 5$<br>The student bought **5 tickets**. | Solve the equation for $x$. |

2) Kelly is selling shirts for her school swim team. There are two prices: a student price and a nonstudent price. During the first week of the sale, Kelly raised $84 by selling 10 shirts to students and 4 shirts to nonstudents. She earned $185 in the second week by selling 20 shirts to students and 10 shirts to nonstudents. What is the student price for a shirt?

**Answer:**

| | |
|---|---|
| Student price = $s$<br>Nonstudent price = $n$ | Assign variables. |

| | |
|---|---|
| $10s + 4n = 84$ <br> $20s + 10n = 185$ | Create two equations using the number of shirts Kelly sold and the money she earned. |
| $10s + 4n = 84$ <br> $10n = -20s + 185$ <br> $n = -2s + 18.5$ <br> $10s + 4(-2s + 18.5) = 84$ <br> $10s - 8s + 74 = 84$ <br> $2s + 74 = 84$ <br> $2s = 10$ <br> $s = 5$ | Solve the system of equations using substitution. |
| The student cost for shirts is **$5**. | |

# Linear Inequalities

## Solving Linear Inequalities

An inequality shows the relationship between two expressions, much like an equation. However, the equal sign is replaced with an inequality symbol that expresses the following relationships:

- ◆ $<$ less than
- ◆ $\leq$ less than or equal to
- ◆ $>$ greater than
- ◆ $\geq$ greater than or equal to

Inequalities are read from left to right. For example, the inequality $x \leq 8$ would be read as "$x$ is less than or equal to 8," meaning $x$ has a value smaller than or equal to 8. The set of solutions of an inequality can be expressed using a number line. The shaded region on the number line represents the set of all the numbers that make an inequality true. One major difference between equations and inequalities is that equations generally have a finite number of solutions, while inequalities generally have infinitely many solutions (an entire interval on the number line containing infinitely many values).

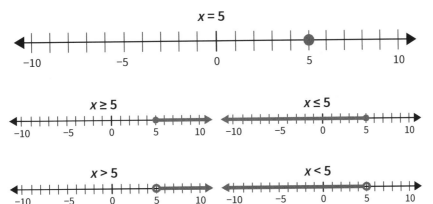

Figure 2.3. Inequalities on a Number Line

Linear inequalities can be solved in the same way as linear equations, with one exception. When multiplying or dividing both sides of an inequality by a negative number, the direction of the inequality sign must reverse—"greater than" becomes "less than" and "less than" becomes "greater than."

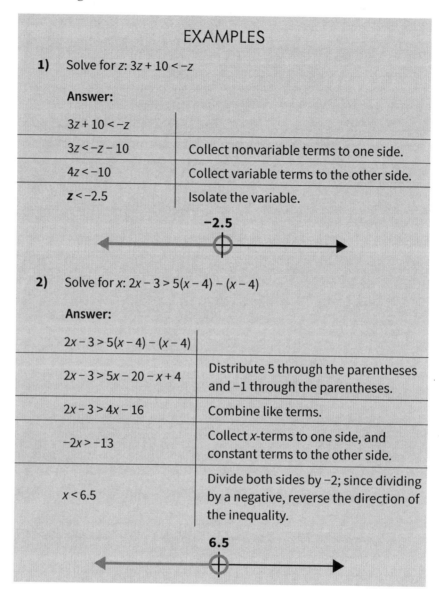

**EXAMPLES**

**1)** Solve for $z$: $3z + 10 < -z$

**Answer:**

| $3z + 10 < -z$ | |
| --- | --- |
| $3z < -z - 10$ | Collect nonvariable terms to one side. |
| $4z < -10$ | Collect variable terms to the other side. |
| $z < -2.5$ | Isolate the variable. |

**2)** Solve for $x$: $2x - 3 > 5(x - 4) - (x - 4)$

**Answer:**

| $2x - 3 > 5(x - 4) - (x - 4)$ | |
| --- | --- |
| $2x - 3 > 5x - 20 - x + 4$ | Distribute 5 through the parentheses and −1 through the parentheses. |
| $2x - 3 > 4x - 16$ | Combine like terms. |
| $-2x > -13$ | Collect $x$-terms to one side, and constant terms to the other side. |
| $x < 6.5$ | Divide both sides by −2; since dividing by a negative, reverse the direction of the inequality. |

# Compound Inequalities

Compound inequalities have more than one inequality expression. Solutions of compound inequalities are the sets of all numbers that make *all* the inequalities true. Some compound inequalities may not have any solutions, some will have solutions that contain some part of the number line, and some will have solutions that include the entire number line.

Table 2.1. Unions and Intersections

| Inequality | Meaning in Words | Number Line |
|---|---|---|
| $a < x < b$ | All values $x$ that are greater than $a$ and less than $b$ | 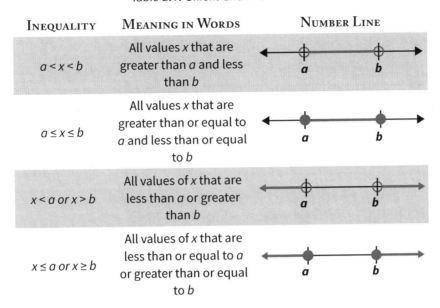 |
| $a \le x \le b$ | All values $x$ that are greater than or equal to $a$ and less than or equal to $b$ | |
| $x < a$ or $x > b$ | All values of $x$ that are less than $a$ or greater than $b$ | |
| $x \le a$ or $x \ge b$ | All values of $x$ that are less than or equal to $a$ or greater than or equal to $b$ | |

Compound inequalities can be written, solved, and graphed as two separate inequalities. For compound inequalities in which the word *and* is used, the solution to the compound inequality will be the set of numbers on the number line where both inequalities have solutions (where both are shaded). For compound inequalities where *or* is used, the solution to the compound inequality will be *all* the shaded regions for *either* inequality.

## EXAMPLES

**1)** Solve the compound inequalities: $2x + 4 < -18$ or $4(x + 2) > 18$

**Answer:**

$2x + 4 < -10$ or $4(x + 2) > 18$

| | |
|---|---|
| $2x < -14 \qquad 4x + 8 > 18$ | |
| $x < -7 \qquad 4x > 10$ | Solve each inequality independently. |
| $\qquad\quad x > 2.5$ | |

The solution to the original compound inequality is **the set of all $x$ for which $x < -7$ or $x > 2.5$.**

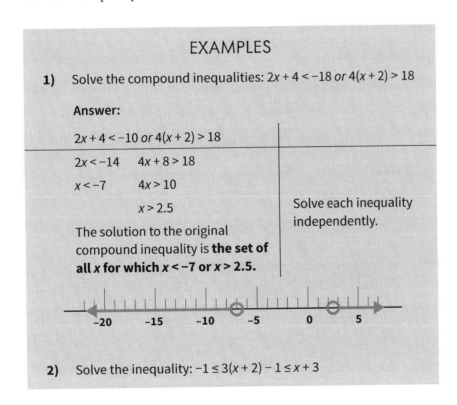

**2)** Solve the inequality: $-1 \le 3(x + 2) - 1 \le x + 3$

**Answer:**

| | |
|---|---|
| $-1 \le 3(x+2) - 1 \le x + 3$ | |
| $-1 \le 3(x+2) - 1$ *and*<br><br>$3(x+2) - 1 \le x + 3$ | Break up the compound inequality into two inequalities. |
| $\begin{aligned} -1 &\le 3x + 6 - 1 \\ -6 &\le 3x \\ -2 &\le x \end{aligned}$ $\quad$ $\begin{aligned} 3x + 6 - 1 &\le x + 3 \\ 2x &\le -2 \end{aligned}$<br><br>$\text{and}\ x \le -1$ | Solve separately. |
| $\mathbf{-2 \le x \le -1}$ | The only values of *x* that satisfy *both* inequalities are the values between −2 and −1 (inclusive). |

# Graphing Linear Inequalities in Two Variables

Linear inequalities in two variables can be graphed in much the same way as linear equations. Start by graphing the corresponding equation of a line (temporarily replace the inequality with an equal sign, and then graph). This line creates a boundary line of two half-planes. If the inequality is a "greater/less than," the boundary should not be included and a dotted line is used. A solid line is used to indicate that the boundary should be included in the solution when the inequality is "greater/less than or equal to."

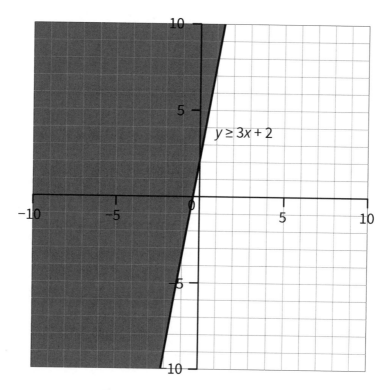

Figure 2.4. Graphing Inequalities

One side of the boundary is the set of all points $(x, y)$ that make the inequality true. This side is shaded to indicate that all these values are solutions. If $y$ is greater than the expression containing $x$, shade above the line; if it is less than, shade below. A point can also be used to check which side of the line to shade.

A set of two or more linear inequalities is a **SYSTEM OF INEQUAL-ITIES**. Solutions to the system are all the values of the variables that make every inequality in the system true. Systems of inequalities are solved graphically by graphing all the inequalities in the same plane. The region where all the shaded solutions overlap is the solution to the system.

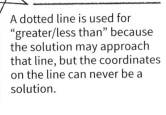

A dotted line is used for "greater/less than" because the solution may approach that line, but the coordinates on the line can never be a solution.

## EXAMPLES

**1)** What is the inequality represented on the graph below?

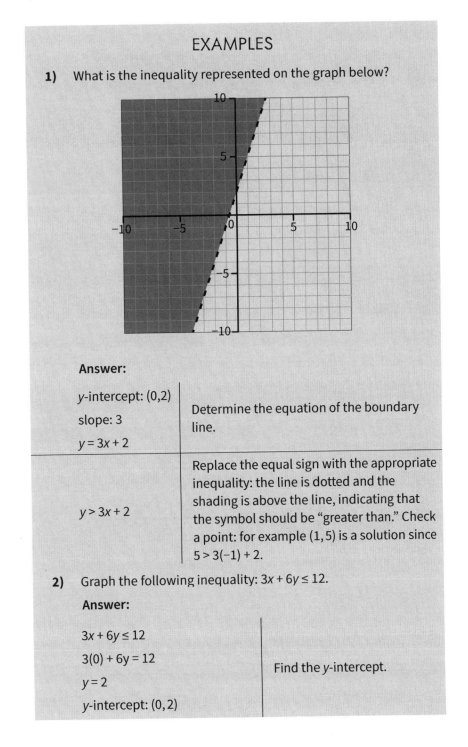

**Answer:**

| | |
|---|---|
| $y$-intercept: (0,2)<br>slope: 3<br>$y = 3x + 2$ | Determine the equation of the boundary line. |
| $y > 3x + 2$ | Replace the equal sign with the appropriate inequality: the line is dotted and the shading is above the line, indicating that the symbol should be "greater than." Check a point: for example $(1, 5)$ is a solution since $5 > 3(-1) + 2$. |

**2)** Graph the following inequality: $3x + 6y \leq 12$.

**Answer:**

| | |
|---|---|
| $3x + 6y \leq 12$<br>$3(0) + 6y = 12$<br>$y = 2$<br>$y$-intercept: (0,2) | Find the $y$-intercept. |

| | |
|---|---|
| $3x + 6(0) \leq 12$<br><br>$x = 4$<br><br>$x$-intercept: $(4, 0)$ | Find the $x$-intercept. |

Graph the line using the intercepts, and shade below the line.

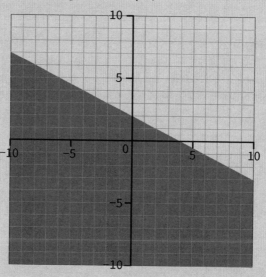

3) Graph the system of inequalities: $-x + y \leq 1, x \geq -1, y > 2x - 4$

**Answer:**

To solve the system, graph all three inequalities in the same plane; then identify the area where the three solutions overlap. All points $(x, y)$ in this area will be solutions to the system since they satisfy all three inequalities.

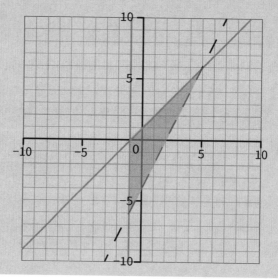

# Quadratic Equations and Inequalities

Quadratic equations are degree 2 polynomials; the highest power on the dependent variable is two. While linear functions are represented graphically as lines, the graph of a quadratic function is a PARABOLA. The graph of a parabola has three important components. The VERTEX is where the graph changes direction. In the parent graph $y = x^2$, the origin $(0, 0)$ is the vertex. The AXIS OF SYMMETRY is the vertical line that cuts the graph into two equal halves. The line of symmetry always passes through the vertex. On the parent graph, the $y$-axis is the axis of symmetry. The ZEROS or ROOTS of the quadratic are the $x$-intercepts of the graph.

## Forms of Quadratic Equations

Quadratic equations can be expressed in two forms:

- **STANDARD FORM: $y = ax^2 + bx + c$**

  Axis of symmetry: $x = -\frac{b}{2a}$      Vertex: $(-\frac{b}{2a}, f(-\frac{b}{2a}))$

- **VERTEX FORM: $y = a(x - h)^2 + k$**

  Vertex: $(h, k)$      Axis of symmetry: $x = h$

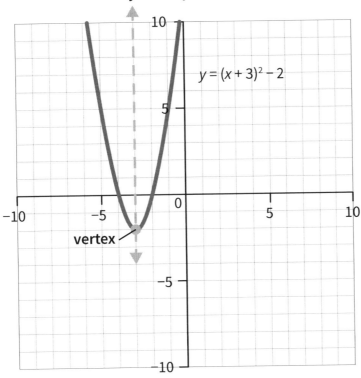

**axis of symmetry**

$y = (x + 3)^2 - 2$

**vertex**

**Figure 2.5. Parabola**

In both equations, the sign of $a$ determines which direction the parabola opens: if $a$ is positive, then it opens upward; if $a$ is negative, then it opens downward. The wideness or narrowness is also determined by $a$. If the absolute value of $a$ is less than one (a proper fraction), then the parabola will get wider the closer $|a|$ is to zero. If the absolute value of $a$ is greater than one, then the larger $|a|$ becomes, the narrower the parabola will be.

Equations in vertex form can be converted to standard form by squaring out the $(x - h)^2$ part (using FOIL), distributing the $a$, adding $k$, and simplifying the result.

Equations can be converted from standard form to vertex form by COMPLETING THE SQUARE. Take an equation in standard form, $y = ax^2 + bc + c$.

1. Move $c$ to the left side of the equation.
2. Divide the entire equation through by $a$ (to make the coefficient of $x^2$ be 1).
3. Take half of the coefficient of $x$, square that number, and then add the result to both sides of the equation.
4. Convert the right side of the equation to a perfect binomial squared, $(x + m)^2$.
5. Isolate $y$ to put the equation in proper vertex form.

## EXAMPLES

1) What is the line of symmetry for $y = -2(x + 3)^2 + 2$?

**Answer:**

This quadratic is given in vertex form, with $h = -3$ and $k = 2$. The vertex of this equation is $(-3, 2)$. The line of symmetry is the vertical line that passes through this point. Since the $x$-value of the point is $-3$, the line of symmetry is $x = -3$.

2) What is the vertex of the parabola $y = -3x^2 + 24x - 27$?

**Answer:**

| | |
|---|---|
| $y = -3x^2 + 24x - 27$ | |
| $x = -\dfrac{b}{2a}$ where $a = -3$, $b = 24$<br>$x = -\dfrac{24}{2(-3)} = 4$ | This quadratic equation is in standard form. Use the formula for finding the $x$-value of the vertex. |
| $y = -3(4)^2 + 24(4) - 27 = 21$<br>The vertex is at **(4, 21)**. | Plug $x = 4$ into the original equation to find the corresponding $y$-value. |

3) Write $y = -3x^2 + 24x - 27$ in vertex form by completing the square.

**Answer:**

| | |
|---|---|
| $y = -3x^2 + 24x - 27$ | |
| $y + 27 = -3x^2 + 24x$ | Move $c$ to the other side of the equation. |

| | |
|---|---|
| $\dfrac{y}{-3} - 9 = x^2 - 8x$ | Divide through by $a$ (–3 in this example). |
| $\dfrac{y}{-3} - 9 + 16 = x^2 - 8x + 16$ | Take half of the new $b$, square it, and add that quantity to both sides: $\frac{1}{2}(-8) = -4$. Squaring it gives $(-4)^2 = 16$. |
| $\dfrac{y}{-3} + 7 = (x - 4)^2$ | Simplify the left side, and write the right side as a binomial squared. |
| $y = -3(x - 4)^2 + 21$ | Subtract 7, and then multiply through by –3 to isolate $y$. |

## Solving Quadratic Equations

Solving the quadratic equation $ax^2 + bx + c = 0$ finds $x$-intercepts of the parabola (by making $y = 0$). These are also called the ROOTS or ZEROS of the quadratic function. A quadratic equation may have zero, one, or two real solutions. There are several ways of finding the zeros. One way is to factor the quadratic into a product of two binomials, and then use the zero product property. (If $m \times n = 0$, then either $m = 0$ or $n = 0$.) Another way is to complete the square and square root both sides. One way that works every time is to memorize and use the QUADRATIC FORMULA:

$$x = \frac{-b \pm \sqrt{b^2 - 4ac}}{2a}$$

The $a$, $b$, and $c$ come from the standard form of quadratic equations above. (Note that to use the quadratic equation, the right-hand side of the equation must be equal to zero.)

The part of the formula under the square root radical ($b^2 - 4ac$) is known as the DISCRIMINANT. The discriminant tells how many and what type of roots will result without actually calculating the roots.

With all graphing problems, putting the function into the $y =$ window of a graphing calculator will aid the process of elimination when graphs are examined and compared to answer choices with a focus on properties like axis of symmetry, vertices, and roots of formulas.

Table 2.2. Discriminants

| IF $B^2 - 4AC$ IS | THERE WILL BE | AND THE PARABOLA |
|---|---|---|
| zero | only 1 real root | has its vertex on the $x$-axis |
| positive | 2 real roots | has **two** $x$-intercepts |
| negative | 0 real roots 2 complex roots | has **no** $x$-intercepts |

## EXAMPLES

1) Find the zeros of the quadratic equation: $y = -(x + 3)^2 + 1$.

**Answer:**

Method 1: Make $y = 0$; isolate $x$ by square rooting both sides:

| | |
|---|---|
| $0 = -(x + 3)^2 + 1$ | Make $y = 0$. |

| | |
|---|---|
| $-1 = -(x + 3)^2$ | Subtract 1 from both sides. |
| $1 = (x + 3)^2$ | Divide by $-1$ on both sides. |
| $(x + 3) = \pm 1$ | Square root both sides. Don't forget to write plus OR minus 1. |
| $(x + 3) = 1 \; or \; (x + 3) = -1$ | Write two equations using $+1$ and $-1$. |
| $x = -2 \; or \; x = -4$ | Solve both equations. These are the zeros. |

Method 2: Convert vertex form to standard form, and then use the quadratic formula.

| | |
|---|---|
| $y = -(x + 3)^2 + 1$ $y = -(x^2 + 6x + 9) + 1$ $y = -x^2 - 6x - 8$ | Put the equation in standard form by distributing and combining like terms. |
| $x = \dfrac{-b \pm \sqrt{(b^2 - 4ac)}}{2a}$ $x = \dfrac{-(-6) \pm \sqrt{(-6)^2 - 4(-1)(-8)}}{2(-1)}$ $x = \dfrac{6 \pm \sqrt{36 - 32}}{-2}$ $x = \dfrac{6 \pm \sqrt{4}}{-2}$ $x = -4, -2$ | Find the zeros using the quadratic formula. |

2) Find the root(s) for: $z^2 - 4z + 4 = 0$

**Answer:**

This polynomial can be factored in the form $(z - 2)(z - 2) = 0$, so the only root is $z = 2$. There is only one $x$-intercept, and the vertex of the graph is *on* the $x$-axis.

3) Write a quadratic function that has zeros at $x = -3$ and $x = 2$ that passes through the point $(-2, 8)$.

**Answer:**

If the quadratic has zeros at $x = -3$ and $x = 2$, then it has factors of $(x + 3)$ and $(x - 2)$. The quadratic function can be written in the factored form $y = a(x + 3)(x - 2)$. To find the $a$-value, plug in the point $(-2, 8)$ for $x$ and $y$:

$8 = a(-2 + 3)(-2 - 2)$

$8 = a(-4)$

$a = -2$

The quadratic function is $y = -2(x + 3)(x - 2)$.

# Graphing Quadratic Equations

The final expected quadratic skills are graphing a quadratic function given its equation and determining the equation of a quadratic function from its graph. The equation's form determines which quantities are easiest to obtain:

Table 2.3 Obtaining Quantities from Quadratic Functions

| NAME OF FORM | EQUATION OF QUADRATIC | EASIEST QUANTITY TO FIND | HOW TO FIND OTHER QUANTITIES |
|---|---|---|---|
| vertex form | $y = a(x-h)^2 + k$ | vertex at $(h, k)$ and axis of symmetry $x = h$ | Find zeros by making $y = 0$ and solving for $x$. |
| factored form | $y = a(x-m)(x-n)$ | $x$ – intercepts at $x = m$ and $x = n$ | Find axis of symmetry by averaging $m$ and $n$: $x = \frac{m+n}{2}$. This is also the $x$-value of the vertex. |
| standard form | $y = ax^2 + bx + c$ | $y$ – intercept at $(0, c)$ | Find axis of symmetry and $x$-value of the vertex using $x = \frac{-b}{2a}$. Find zeros using quadratic formula. |

To graph a quadratic function, first determine if the graph opens up or down by examining the $a$-value. Then determine the quantity that is easiest to find based on the form given, and find the vertex. Then other values can be found, if necessary, by choosing $x$-values and finding the corresponding $y$-values. Using symmetry instantly doubles the number of points that are known.

Given the graph of a parabola, the easiest way to write a quadratic equation is to identify the vertex and insert the $h$- and $k$-values into the vertex form of the equation. The $a$-value can be determined by finding another point the graph goes through, plugging these values in for $x$ and $y$, and solving for $a$.

## EXAMPLES

1) Graph the quadratic $y = 2(x-3)^2 + 4$.

**Answer:**

Start by marking the vertex at (3, 4) and recognizing this parabola opens upward. The line of symmetry is $x = 3$. Now, plug in an easy value for $x$ to get one point on the curve; then use symmetry to find another point. In this case, choose $x = 2$ (one unit to the left of the line of symmetry) and solve for $y$:

$$y = 2(2-3)^2 + 4$$
$$y = 2(1) + 4$$
$$y = 6$$

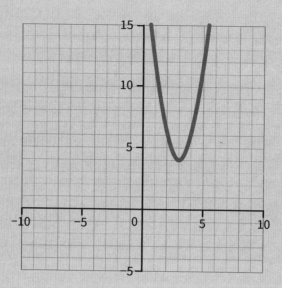

Thus the point $(2, 6)$ is on the curve. Then use symmetry to find the corresponding point one unit to the right of the line of symmetry, which must also have a $y$ value of 6. This point is $(4, 6)$. Draw a parabola through the points.

2) What is the vertex form of the equation shown on the following graph?

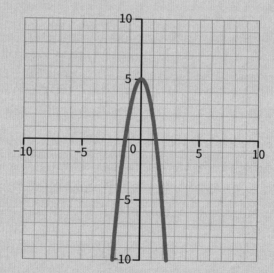

**Answer:**

$(h, k) = (0, 5)$

$y = a(x - h)^2 + k$

$y = a(x - 0)^2 + 5$

$y = ax^2 + 5$

Locate the vertex and plug values for $h$ and $k$ into the vertex form of the quadratic equation.

| | |
|---|---|
| $(x, y) = (1, 2)$<br>$y = ax^2 + 5$<br>$2 = a(1)^2 + 5$<br>$a = -3$ | Choose another point on the graph to plug into this equation to solve for $a$. |
| $y = -3x^2 + 5$ | Plug $a$ into the vertex form of the equation. |

## Quadratic Inequalities

Quadratic inequalities with two variables, such as $y < (x + 3)^2 - 2$ can be graphed much like linear inequalities: graph the equation by treating the inequality symbol as an equal sign, then shade the graph. Shade above the graph when $y$ is greater is than, and below the graph when $y$ is less than.

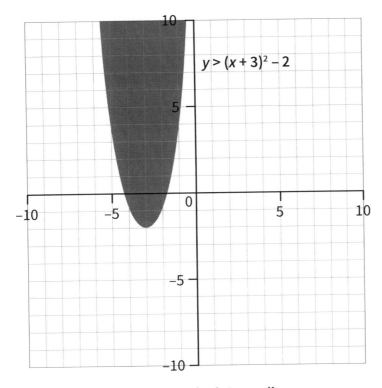

**Figure 2.6. Quadratic Inequality**

Quadratic inequalities with only one variable, such as $x^2 - 4x > 12$, can be solved by first manipulating the inequality so that one side is zero. The zeros can then be found and used to determine where the inequality is greater than zero (positive) or less than zero (negative). Often it helps to set up intervals on a number line and test a value within each range created by the zeros to identify the values that create positive or negative values.

## EXAMPLE

Find the values of $x$ such that $x^2 - 4x > 12$.

**Answer:**

| | |
|---|---|
| $x^2 - 4x = 12$<br>$x^2 - 4x - 12 = 0$<br>$(x + 2)(x - 6) = 0$<br>$x = -2, 6$ | Find the zeros of the inequality. |

| $x$ | $(x + 2)(x - 6)$ | Create a table or number line with the intervals created by the zeros. Use a test value to determine whether the expression is positive or negative. |
|---|---|---|
| $-\infty < x < -2$ | + | |
| $-2 < x < 6$ | – | |
| $6 < x < \infty$ | + | |

| | |
|---|---|
| $x < -2$ or $x > 6$ | Identify the values of $x$ which make the expression positive. |

# Functions

## Working with Functions

Functions can be thought of as a process: when something is put in, an action (or operation) is performed, and something different comes out. A **FUNCTION** is a relationship between two quantities (for example $x$ and $y$) in which, for every value of the independent variable (usually $x$), there is exactly one value of the dependent variable (usually $y$). Briefly, each input has *exactly one* output. Graphically this means the graph passes the **VERTICAL LINE TEST**: anywhere a vertical line is drawn on the graph, the line hits the curve at exactly one point.

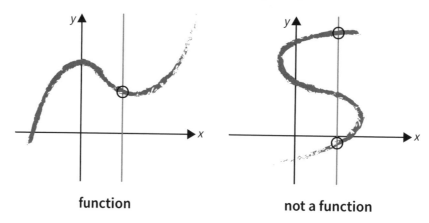

function                    not a function

**Figure 2.7. Vertical Line Test**

The notation $f(x)$ or $g(t)$, etc., is often used when a function is being considered. This is **FUNCTION NOTATION**. The input value is $x$ and the output value $y$ is written as $y = f(x)$. Thus, $f(2)$ represents the output value (or *y* value) when *x* = 2, and *f*(2) = 5 means that when *x* = 2 is plugged into the *f*(*x*) function, the output (*y* value) is 5. In other words, *f*(2) = 5 represents the point (2, 5) on the graph of *f*(*x*).

Every function has an **INPUT DOMAIN** and **OUTPUT RANGE**. The domain is the set of all the possible *x* values that can be used as input values (these are found along the horizontal axis on the graph), and the range includes all the *y* values or output values that result from applying *f*(*x*) (these are found along the vertical axis on the graph). Domain and range are usually intervals of numbers and are often expressed as inequalities, such as *x* < 2 (the domain is all values less than 2) or 3 < *x* < 15 (all values between 3 and 15).

Interval notation can also be used to show domain and range. Round brackets indicate that an end value is not included, and square brackets show that it is. The symbol ∪ means *or*, and the symbol ∩ means *and*. For example, the statement (–infinity, 4) ∪ (4, infinity) describes the set of all real numbers except 4.

A function *f*(*x*) is **EVEN** if *f*(–*x*) = *f*(*x*). Even functions have symmetry across the *y*-axis. An example of an even function is the parent quadratic *y* = *x*², because any value of *x* (for example, 3) and its opposite –*x* (for example, –3) have the same *y* value (for example, 3² = 9 and (–3)² = 9). A function is **ODD** if *f*(–*x*) = –*f*(*x*). Odd functions have symmetry about the origin. For example, *f*(*x*) = *x*³ is an odd function because *f*(3) = 27, and *f*(–3) = –27. A function may be even, odd, or neither.

**even**        **odd**

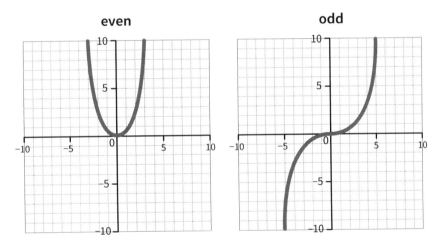

Figure 2.8. Even and Odd Functions

## EXAMPLES

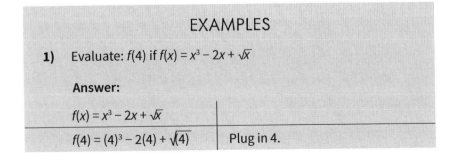

**1)** Evaluate: $f(4)$ if $f(x) = x^3 - 2x + \sqrt{x}$

**Answer:**

| $f(x) = x^3 - 2x + \sqrt{x}$ | |
|---|---|
| $f(4) = (4)^3 - 2(4) + \sqrt{(4)}$ | Plug in 4. |

$= 64 - 8 + 2$

$= \textbf{58}$

Follow the PEMDAS order of operations.

**2)** What are the domain and range of the following function?

**Answer:**

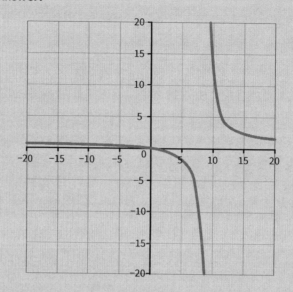

This function has an asymptote at $x = 9$, so is not defined there. Otherwise, the function is defined for all other values of $x$.

**D:** $-\infty < x < \textbf{9}$ or $\textbf{9} < x < \infty$

Since the function has a horizontal asymptote at $y = 1$ that it never crosses, the function never takes the value 1, so the range is all real numbers except 1: **R:** $-\infty < y < 1 \, or \, 1 < y < \infty$.

**3)** Which of the following represents a function?

A.

| $x$ | $g(x)$ |
|---|---|
| 0 | 0 |
| 1 | 1 |
| 2 | 2 |
| 1 | 3 |

B.

| $x$ | $f(x)$ |
|---|---|
| 0 | 1 |
| 0 | 2 |
| 0 | 3 |
| 0 | 4 |

C.

| $t$ | $f(t)$ |
|---|---|
| 1 | 1 |
| 2 | 2 |
| 3 | 3 |
| 4 | 4 |

D.

| $x$ | $f(x)$ |
|---|---|
| 0 | 0 |
| 5 | 1 |
| 0 | 2 |
| 5 | 3 |

Put any function into the $y =$ part of a calculator and look at the table to get domain and range values. Looking at $-100, -10, 0, 10,$ and $100$ give a sense about any function's limitations.

**Answer:**

For a set of numbers to represent a function, every input must generate a unique output. Therefore, if the same input ($x$) appears more than once in the table, determine if that input has two different outputs. If so, then the table does not represent a function.

A.  This table is not a function because input value 1 has two different outputs (1 and 3).

B.  Table B is not function because 0 is the only input and results in four different values.

C.  This table shows a function because each input has one output.

D.  This table also has one input going to two different values, so it is not a function.

**4)**  What is the domain and the range of the following graph?

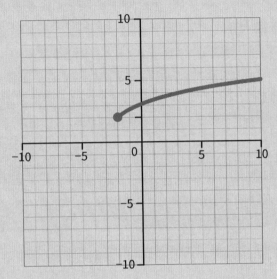

**Answer:**

For the domain, this graph goes on to the right to positive infinity. Its leftmost point, however, is $x = -2$. Therefore, its domain is all real numbers equal to or greater than $-2$, **D: $-2 \leq x < \infty$**, or **$[-2, \infty)$**.

The lowest range value is $y = 2$. Although it has a decreasing slope, this function continues to rise. Therefore, the domain is all real numbers greater than 2, **R: $2 \leq y < \infty$ or $[2, \infty)$**.

# Average Rate of Change of Functions

The average rate of change of a functions $f(x)$ over an interval $[a, b]$ is the slope of the line connecting the points $(a, f(a))$ and $(b, f(b))$. It is how much the $y$-value changes, on average, for every change of 1 unit in $x$ on the interval:

$$\text{Average value of } f(x) = \frac{f(b) - f(a)}{b - a}$$

### EXAMPLE

Find the average rate of change of the function $f(x) = \sqrt{x-1}$ over the interval $[5, 17]$.

Inverse graphs can be tested by taking any point on one graph and flipping coordinates to see if that new point is on the other curve. For example, the coordinate point (5, −2) is on the function and (−2, 5) is a point on its inverse.

## Inverse Functions

INVERSE FUNCTIONS switch the inputs and the outputs of a function. If $f(x) = k$ then the inverse of that function would read $f^{-1}(k) = x$. The domain of $f^{-1}(x)$ is the range of $f(x)$, and the range of $f^{-1}(x)$ is the domain of $f(x)$. If point $(a, b)$ is on the graph of $f(x)$, then point $(b, a)$ will be on the graph of $f^{-1}(x)$. Because of this fact, the graph of $f^{-1}(x)$ is a reflection of the graph of $f(x)$ across the line $y = x$. Inverse functions "undo" all the operations of the original function.

The steps for finding an inverse function are:

1. Replace $f(x)$ with $y$ to make it easier manipulate the equation.
2. Switch the $x$ and $y$.
3. Solve for $y$.
4. Label the inverse function as $f^{-1}(x) =$.

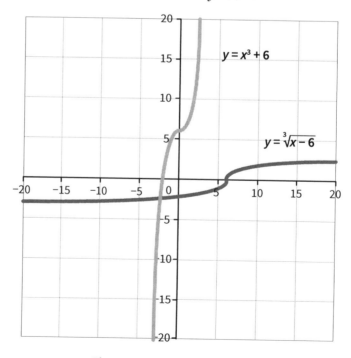

Figure 2.9. Inverse Functions

# EXAMPLESS

**1)** Find the inverse of the graph of $f(x) = -1 - \frac{1}{5}x$

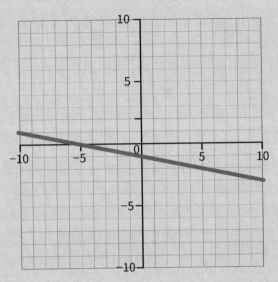

**Answer:**

This is a linear graph with some clear coordinates: $(-5, 0)$, $(0, -1)$, $(5, -2)$, and $(10, -3)$. This means the inverse function will have coordinate $(0, -5)$, $(-1, 0)$, $(-2, 5)$, and $(-3, 10)$. The inverse function is reflected over the line $y = x$ and is the line $f^{-1}(x) = -5(x + 1)$ below.

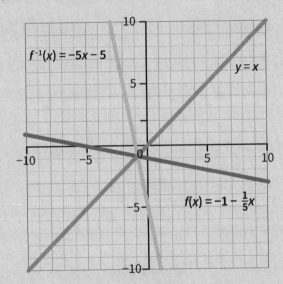

**2)** What is the inverse of function of $f(x) = 5x + 5$?

**Answer:**

| $y = 5x + 5$ | Replace $f(x)$ with $y$ |
|---|---|
| $x = 5y + 5$ | Switch the places of $y$ and $x$. |

| | |
|---|---|
| $x = 5y + 5$ | |
| $x - 5 = 5y$ | Solve for $y$. |
| $y = \frac{x}{5} - 1$ | |
| $f^{-1}(x) = \frac{x}{5} - 1$ | |

# Compound Functions

COMPOUND FUNCTIONS take two or more functions and combine them using operations or composition. Functions can be combined using addition, subtraction, multiplication, or division:

$$\text{addition: } (f + g)(x) = f(x) + g(x)$$

$$\text{subtraction: } (f - g)(x) = f(x) - g(x)$$

$$\text{multiplication: } (fg)(x) = f(x)g(x)$$

$$\text{division: } \left(\frac{f}{g}\right)(x) = \frac{f(x)}{g(x)} \ \text{ (note that } g(x) \neq 0)$$

Functions can also be combined using COMPOSITION. Composition of functions is indicated by the notation $(f \circ g)(x)$. Note that the $\circ$ symbol does NOT mean multiply. It means take the output of $g(x)$ and make it the input of $f(x)$:

$$(f \circ g)(x) = f(g(x))$$

This equation is read $f$ of $g$ of x, and will be a new function of $x$. Note that order is important. In general, $f(g(x)) \neq g(f(x))$. They *will* be equal when $f(x)$ and $g(x)$ are inverses of each other, however, as both will simplify to the original input $x$. This is because performing a function on a value and then using that output as the input to the inverse function should bring you back to the original value.

The domain of a composition function is the set of $x$ values that are in the domain of the "inside" function $g(x)$ such that $g(x)$ is in the domain of the outside function $f(x)$. For example, if $f(x) = \frac{1}{x}$ and $g(x) = \sqrt{x}$, $f(g(x))$ has a domain of $x > 0$ because $g(x)$ has a domain of $x \geq 0$. But when $f(x)$ is applied to the $\sqrt{x}$ function, the composition function becomes $\frac{1}{\sqrt{x}}$ and the value $x = 0$ is no longer allowed because it would result in 0 in the denominator, so the domain must be further restricted.

## EXAMPLES

1) If $z(x) = 3x - 3$ and $y(x) = 2x - 1$, find $(y \circ z)(-4)$.

   **Answer:**

   | | |
   |---|---|
   | $(y \circ z)(-4) = y(z(-4))$ | |
   | $z(-4)$ | |
   | $= 3(-4) - 3$ | Starting on the inside, evaluate $z$. |
   | $= -12 - 3$ | |
   | $= -15$ | |

$$y(z(-4))$$

$$= y(-15)$$

$$= 2(-15) - 1 \qquad \text{Replace } z(-4) \text{ with } -15, \text{ and simplify.}$$

$$= -30 - 1$$

$$= \mathbf{-31}$$

**2)** Find $(k \circ t)(x)$ if $k(x) = \frac{1}{2}x - 3$ and $t(x) = \frac{1}{2}x - 2$.

**Answer:**

| | |
|---|---|
| $(k \circ t)(x) = k(t(x))$ | |
| $= k\left(\frac{1}{2}x - 2\right)$ | Replace $x$ in the $k(x)$ function with $\left(\frac{1}{2}x - 2\right)$ |
| $= \frac{1}{2}\left(\frac{1}{2}x - 2\right) - 3$ | |
| $= \frac{1}{4}x - 1 - 3$ | Simplify. |
| $= \frac{1}{4}x - 4$ | |
| $(k \circ t)(x) = \frac{1}{4}x - 4$ | |

**3)** The wait ($W$) in minutes to get on a ride at an amusement park depends on the number of people ($N$) in the park. The number of people in the park depends on the number of hours, $t$, that the park has been open. Suppose $N(t) = 400t$ and $W(N) = 5(1.2)\frac{N}{100}$. What is the value and the meaning in context of $N(4)$ and $W(N(4))$?

**Answer:**

$N(4) = 400(4) = 1600$ and means that 4 hours after the park opens there are 1600 people in the park. $W(N(4)) = W(1600) = 96$ and means that 4 hours after the park opens the wait time is about **96 minutes** for the ride.

# Exponential Functions

An **EXPONENTIAL FUNCTION** has a constant base and a variable in the exponent: $f(x) = b^x$ is an exponential function with base $b$ and exponent $x$. The value $b$ is the quantity that the $y$ value is multiplied by each time the $x$ value is increased by 1. When looking at a table of values, an exponential function can be identified because the $f(x)$ values are being multiplied. (In contrast, linear $f(x)$ values are being added to.)

The graph of the exponential parent function does not cross the $x$-axis, which is the function's horizontal asymptote. The $y$-intercept of the function is at $(0, 1)$.

The general formula for an exponential function, $f(x) = ab^{(x-h)} + k$, allows for transformations to be made to the function. The value

To solve an exponential equation, start by looking for a common base:
$4^{x-2} = \sqrt{8}$
can be rewritten as
$(2^2)^{(x-2)} = (2^3)^{\frac{1}{2}}$
If no common base can be found, logarithms can be used to move the variable out of the exponent position.

*h* moves the function left or right (moving the *y*-intercept) while the value *k* moves the function up or down (moving both the *y*-intercept and the horizontal asymptote). The value *a* stretches or compresses the function (moving the *y*-intercept).

Exponential equations have at least one variable in an exponent position. One way to solve these equations is to make the bases on both side of the equation equivalent, and then equate the exponents. Many exponential equations do not have a solution. Negative numbers often lead to no solutions: for example, $2^x = -8$. The domain of exponential functions is only positive numbers, as seen above, so there is no *x* value that will result in a negative output.

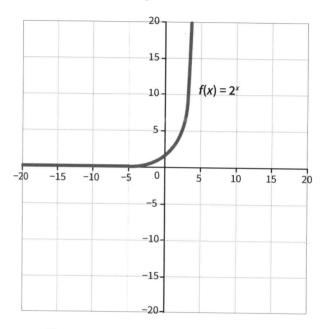

**Figure 2.10. Exponential Parent Function**

---

## EXAMPLES

1) Graph the exponential function $f(x) = 5^x - 2$.

   **Answer:**

   One way to do this is to use a table:

   | $x$ | $5^x - 2$ |
   |:---:|:---:|
   | −2 | $\frac{1}{25} - 2 = -\frac{49}{25}$ |
   | −1 | $\frac{1}{5} - 2 = -\frac{9}{5}$ |
   | 0 | $1 - 2 = -1$ |
   | 1 | $5 - 2 = 3$ |
   | 2 | $25 - 2 = 23$ |

Another way to graph this is simply to see this function as the parent function $y = b^x$ (with $b = 5$), shifted down by a vertical shift of 2 units. Thus the new horizontal asymptote will be at $y = 2$, and the new $y$-intercept will be $y = -1$.

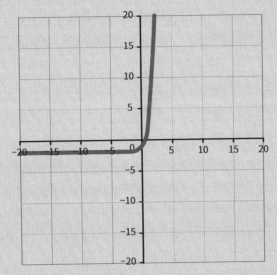

2) If the height of grass in a yard in a humid summer week grows by 5% every day, how much taller would the grass be after six days?

**Answer:**

Any time a question concerns growth or decay, an exponential function must be created to solve it. In this case, create a table with initial value $a$, and a daily growth rate of $(1+0.05) = 1.05$ per day.

| Days ($x$) | Height ($h$) |
|---|---|
| 0 | $a$ |
| 1 | $1.05a$ |
| 2 | $1.05(1.05a) = (1.05)^2a$ |
| 3 | $(1.05)^2(1.05a) = (1.05)^3a$ |
| $x$ | $(1.05)^xa$ |

After six days the height of the grass is $(1.05)^6 = $ **1.34 times as tall**. The grass would grow 34% in one week.

3) Solve for $x$: $4^{x+1} = \frac{1}{256}$

**Answer:**

| | |
|---|---|
| $4^{x+1} = \frac{1}{256}$ | |
| $4^{x+1} = 4^{-4}$ | Find a common base and rewrite the equation. |

| | |
|---|---|
| $x + 1 = -4$ <br> $x = -5$ | Set the exponents equal and solve for $x$. |

## Special Exponential Equations

There are three exponential function formulas that frequently show up in word problems:

The GROWTH FORMULA:

$y = a(1 + r)^t$  Initial amount $a$ increases at a rate of $r$ per time period

The DECAY FORMULA:

$y = a(1 - r)^t$  Initial amount $a$ decreases at a rate of $r$ per time period

In these formulas, $a$ is the initial amount (at time $t = 0$), $r$ is the rate of growth or decay (written as a decimal in the formula), and $t$ is the number of growth or decay cycles that have passed.

A special case of the growth function is known as the COMPOUND-INTEREST FORMULA:

$$A = P\left(1 + \frac{r}{n}\right)^{nt}$$

In this formula, $A$ is the future value of an investment, $P$ is the initial deposit (or principal), $r$ is the interest rate as a percentage, $n$ is the number of times interest is compounded within a time period, or how often interest is applied to the account in a year (once per year, $n = 1$; monthly, $n = 12$; etc.), and $t$ is the number of compounding cycles (usually years).

### EXAMPLES

1) In the year 2000, the number of text messages sent in a small town was 120. If the number of text messages grew every year afterward by 124%, how many years would it take for the number of text messages to surpass 36,000?

**Answer:**

| | |
|---|---|
| $y = a(1 + r)^t$ <br> $36{,}000 = 120(1 + 1.24)^t$ | Plug the given values into the growth equation. |
| $300 = (2.24)^t$ <br> $\log_{2.24} 300 = \log_{2.24}(2.24)^t$ <br> $7.07 \approx t$ <br> The number of text messages will pass 36,000 in **7.07 years**. | Use the properties of logarithms to solve the equation. |

**2)** The half-life of a certain isotope is 5.5 years. If there were 20 grams of one such isotope left after 22 years, what was its original weight?

**Answer:**

| | |
|---|---|
| $t = \frac{22}{5.5} = 4$ <br> $r = 0.5$ <br> $a = ?$ | Identify the variables. |
| $20 = a(1 - 0.50)^4$ <br> $20 = a(0.5)^4$ <br> $20 = a(\frac{1}{2})^4$ <br> $20 = a(\frac{1}{16})$ <br> $320 = a$ <br><br> The original weight is **320 grams**. | Plug these values into the decay formula and solve. |

**3)** If there were a glitch at a bank and a savings account accrued 5% interest five times per week, what would be the amount earned on a $50 deposit after twelve weeks?

**Answer:**

| | |
|---|---|
| $r = 0.05$ <br> $n = 5$ <br> $t = 12$ <br> $P = 50$ | Identify the variables. |
| $A = 50\left(1 + \frac{0.05}{5}\right)^{5(12)}$ <br> $A = 50(1.01)^{60}$ <br> $A = 50(1.82) = 90.83$ | Use the compound-interest formula, since this problem has many steps of growth within a time period. |
| $90.83 - 50$ <br><br> $= \$40.83$ | Subtract the original deposit to find the amount of interest earned. |

# Polynomial and Rational Functions

## Zeros of Polynomial Functions

A polynomial is any equation or expression with two or more terms with whole number exponents. All polynomials with only one variable are functions. The zeros, or roots, of a polynomial function are where the function equals zero and crosses the $x$-axis.

A linear function is a degree 1 polynomial and always has one zero. A quadratic function is a degree 2 polynomial and always has exactly two roots (including complex roots and counting repeated roots separately). This pattern is extended in the **Fundamental Theorem of Algebra**:

**A polynomial function with degree $n > 0$ such as $f(x) = ax^n + bx^{n-1} + cx^{n-2} + \ldots + k$, has exactly $n$ (real or complex) roots (some roots may be repeated)**. Simply stated, whatever the degree of the polynomial is, that is how many roots it will have.

Table 2.4. Zeros of Polynomial Functions

| Polynomial Degree, $N$ | Number and Possible Types of Zeros |
|---|---|
| 1 | 1 real zero (guaranteed) |
| 2 | 0, 1, or 2 real zeros possible<br>2 real **or** complex zeros (guaranteed) |
| 3 | 1, 2, or 3 real zeros possible (there must be at least one real zero)<br>Or 1 real zero (guaranteed) and 2 complex zeros (guaranteed) |
| 4 | 0, 1, 2, 3, or 4 real zeros (possible)<br>Or 2 real zeros and 2 complex zeros or 4 complex zeros |
| … | … |

All the zeros of a polynomial satisfy the equation $f(x) = 0$. That is, if $k$ is a zero of a polynomial, then plugging in $x = k$ into the polynomial results in 0. This also means that the polynomial is evenly divisible by the factor $(x - k)$.

All polynomials where $n$ is an odd number will have at least one real zero or root. Complex zeros always come in pairs (specifically, complex conjugate pairs).

---

### EXAMPLE

Find the roots of the polynomial: $y = 3t^4 - 48$

**Answer:**

| | |
|---|---|
| $y = 3t^4 - 48$ | |
| $3(t^4 - 16) = 0$ | Factor the polynomial. Remove the common factor of 3 from each term and make $y = 0$. |
| $3(t^2 - 4)(t^2 + 4) = 0$<br>$3(t + 2)(t - 2)(t^2 + 2) = 0$ | Factor the difference of squares.<br>$t^2 - 4$ is also a difference of squares. |
| $t + 2 = 0 \quad t - 2 = 0 \quad t^2 + 2 = 0$<br>$t = -2 \quad\quad t = 2 \quad t^2 = -2$<br>$t = \pm\sqrt{2} = \pm 2i$ | Set each factor equal to zero. Solve each equation. |

This degree 4 polynomial has four roots, two real roots: **2 or −2**, and two complex roots: **2*i* or −2*i***. The graph will have two *x*-intercepts at (−2, 0) and (2, 0).

# Graphing Rational Functions

Rations functions are graphed by examining the function to find key features of the graph, including asymptotes, intercepts, and holes.

A **VERTICAL ASYMPTOTE** exists at any value that makes the denominator of a (simplified) rational function equal zero. A vertical asymptote is a vertical line through an *x* value that is not in the domain of the rational function (the function is undefined at this value because division by 0 is not allowed). The function approaches, but never crosses, this line, and the *y* values increase (or decrease) without bound (or "go to infinity") as this *x* value is approached.

To find *x*-intercepts and vertical asymptotes, factor the numerator and denominator of the function. Cancel any terms that appear in the numerator and denominator (if there are any). These values will appear as **HOLES** on the final graph. Since a fraction only equals 0 when its numerator is 0, set the simplified numerator equal to 0 and solve to find the *x*-intercepts. Next, set the denominator equal to 0 and solve to find the vertical asymptotes.

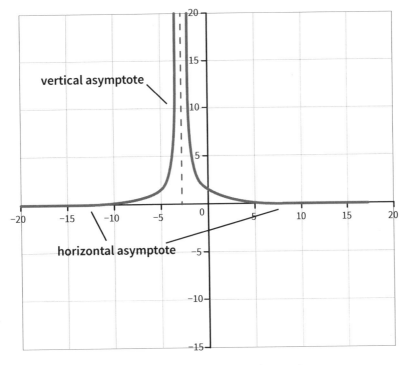

**Figure 2.11. Graphing Rational Functions**

**HORIZONTAL ASYMPTOTES** are horizontal lines that describe the "end behavior" of a rational function. In other words, the horizontal asymptote describes what happens to the $y$-values of the function as the $x$-values get very large ($x \to \infty$) or very small ($x \to -\infty$). A horizontal asymptote occurs if the degree of the numerator of a rational function is less than or equal to the degree in the denominator. The table summarizes the conditions for horizontal asymptotes:

**Table 2.5. Conditions for Horizontal Asymptotes**

For polynomials with first terms $\frac{ax^n}{bx^d}$ ...

| | | |
|---|---|---|
| $n < d$ | as $x \to \infty, y \to 0$ <br> as $x \to -\infty, y \to 0$ | The $x$-axis ($y = 0$) is a horizontal asymptote. |
| $n = d$ | as $x \to \pm\infty, y \to \frac{a}{b}$ | There is a horizontal asymptote at $y = \frac{a}{b}$. |
| $n > d$ | as $x \to \infty, y \to \infty$ or $-\infty$ <br> as $x \to -\infty, y \to \infty$ or $-\infty$ | There is no horizontal asymptote. |

## EXAMPLES

**1)** Create a function that has an $x$-intercept at (5, 0) and vertical asymptotes at $x = 1$ and $x = -1$.

**Answer:**

The numerator will have a factor of $(x - 5)$ in order to have a zero at $x = 5$. The denominator will need factors of $(x - 1)$ and $(x + 1)$ in order for the denominator to be 0 when $x$ is 1 or −1. Thus, one function that would have these features is

$$y = \frac{(x-5)}{(x+1)(x-1)} = \frac{x-5}{x^2-1}$$

**2)** Graph the function: $f(x) = \frac{3x^2 - 12x}{x^2 - 2x - 3}$.

**Answer:**

| | |
|---|---|
| $y = \dfrac{3x^2 - 12x}{x^2 - 2x - 3}$ <br><br> $= \dfrac{3x(x - 4)}{(x - 3)(x + 1)}$ | Factor the equation. |
| $3x(x - 4) = 0$ <br><br> $x = 0, 4$ | Find the roots by setting the numerator equal to zero. |
| $(x - 3)(x + 1) = 0$ <br><br> $x = -1, 3$ | Find the vertical asymptotes by setting the denominator equal to zero. |
| The degree of the numerator and denominator are equal, so the asymptote is the ratio of the coefficients: <br><br> $y = \frac{3}{1} = 3$ | Find the horizontal asymptote by looking at the degree of the numerator and the denominator. |

Use the roots and asymptotes to graph the function.

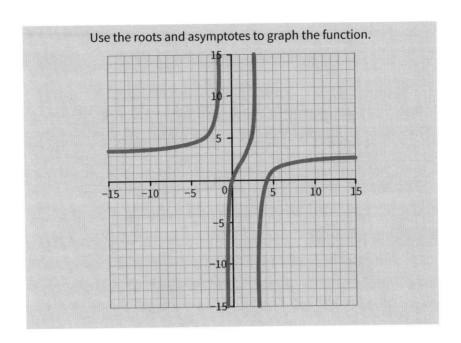

# Modeling Relationships

Modeling relationships requires use of one of four of the function types examined in Table 2.8 with an appropriate equation for a word problem or scenario.

Table 2.6. Function Types

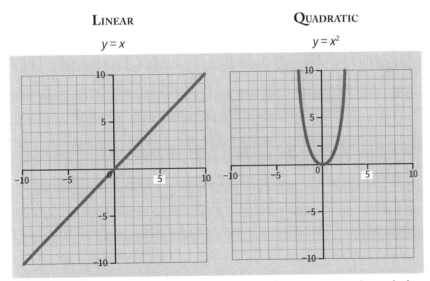

| **LINEAR** | **QUADRATIC** |
| --- | --- |
| $y = x$ | $y = x^2$ |
| Key words: constant change, slope, equal | Key words: area, squared, parabola |

GO ON

Table 2.6. Function Types (continued)

| EXPONENTIAL | LOGARITHMIC |
| --- | --- |
| $y = a^x$ | $y = \log(x)$ |

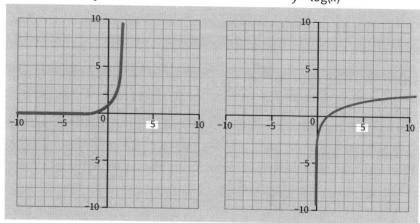

| Key words: growth, decay, interest, double, triple, half-life | Key words: log-scale, base, log equations |
| --- | --- |

Since exponential functions and log functions are inverses of each other, it will often be the case that exponential or log problems can be solved by either type of equation.

## EXAMPLES

1) Consider the following sets of coordinate pairs of a function: {(-1, 0.4), (0, 1), (2, 6.25), and (3, 15.625)}. What kind of function does this represent?

**Answer:**

Graphing on the coordiante plane shows what looks like an exponential function.

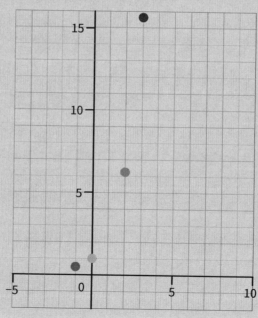

If it is exponential, then its equation is $y = ab^x$, where $a$ is the $y$-intercept, so $a = 1$ in this case. The $b$ is the growth or decay value. Plug in another point, such as $(2, 6.25)$ to solve for $b$:

$$y = ab^x$$

$$6.25 = (1)b^2$$

$$b = \sqrt{6.25} = 2.5$$

The equation, then, is $y = 2.5^x$.

Check another point to confirm: Is $0.4 = 2.5^{-1}$? Since $2.5 = \frac{5}{2}$, and $\left(\frac{5}{2}\right)^{-1} = \frac{2}{5} = 0.4$, the equation works. The function is **exponential**.

2) At a recent sporting event, there were 20,000 people in attendance. When it ended, people left the building at a rate of 1,000 people in the first minute, 1,000 more in the second minute, 1,000 in the third minute, and so on. What equation describes the behavior of attendees leaving the event for every minute after the event finished?

**Answer:**

The dependent variable is the number of attendees leaving the event ($y$). There is a constant change of 1,000 people per minute. Note that this is an additive pattern in the table: every increase of 1 in time results in a subtraction of the same value (1,000) in $y$. Because it is a constant rate of change, a linear model is required:

$$y = 20{,}000 - 1{,}000x$$

Here 20,000 is the $y$-intercept, and the rate of change, –1,000, is the slope.

To test this model, confirm that 18,000 attendees were left in the building after two minutes:

$$y = 20{,}000 - 1{,}000(2) = 18{,}000$$

The model is correct.

# Trigonometry

Trigonometry comes from the Greek words for *triangle* and *measuring*. Appropriately enough, trigonometry is used to find missing angles or side lengths in a triangle. Trigonometric questions often require use of algebraic skills with geometric concepts.

## The Six Trigonometric Functions

There are six different trigonometric functions that are the foundations of trigonometry. They can be thought of as three pairs, as they are reciprocals of one another. All of these functions are ratios of the side lengths of a right triangle. The longest side of a right triangle (opposite the 90-degree angle) is called the HYPOTENUSE. The side

SOHCAHTOA, or Some Old Horse Caught Another Horse Taking Oats Away, is a way to remember that Sine is Opposite over Hypotenuse, Cosine is Adjacent over Hypotenuse, and Tangent is Opposite over Adjacent.

directly opposite the angle being used is the **OPPOSITE**, and the side next to the angle is called the **ADJACENT** side.

Table 2.7. The Six Trigonometric Functions

| Sine Function | Cosine Function | Tangent Function |
|---|---|---|
| $\sin\theta = \dfrac{\text{opposite}}{\text{hypotenuse}}$ | $\cos\theta = \dfrac{\text{adjacent}}{\text{hypotenuse}}$ | $\tan\theta = \dfrac{\text{opposite}}{\text{adjacent}}$ |
| Cosecant Function | Secant Function | Cotangent Function |
| $\csc\theta = \dfrac{\text{hypotenuse}}{\text{opposite}}$ | $\sec\theta = \dfrac{\text{hypotenuse}}{\text{adjacent}}$ | $\cot\theta = \dfrac{\text{adjacent}}{\text{opposite}}$ |

There are a couple of special triangles that are used frequently and whose properties are worth memorizing. They are the 30° – 60° – 90° and the 45° – 45° – 90° triangles.

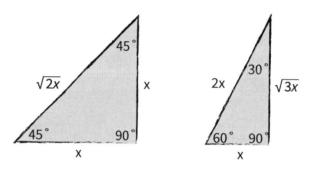

Figure 2.12. **Special Right Triangles**

For the 30° – 60° – 90° triangle, the side opposite the 30° angle (the shortest side) is always half the hypotenuse length, and the medium side (opposite the 60° angle) is $\sqrt{3}$ times the shortest side.

For the 45° – 45° – 90° triangle, two legs have the same length since two angles are equal (the triangle is isosceles), and the hypotenuse is always $\sqrt{2}$ times the length of a leg.

## EXAMPLES

1) Find all six trigonometric ratios for $\theta$ in the following triangle:

**Answer:**

The side directly opposite of $\theta$ is 15. The hypotenuse is the longest side with a length of 17. This leaves the 8 as the adjacent.

| Sine Function | Cosine Function | Tangent Function |
|---|---|---|
| $\sin\theta = \frac{15}{17} = 0.88$ | $\cos\theta = \frac{8}{17} = 0.47$ | $\tan\theta = \frac{15}{8} = 1.88$ |
| Cosecant Function $\csc\theta = \frac{17}{15} = 1.13$ | Secant Function $\sec\theta = \frac{17}{8} = 2.13$ | Cotangent Function $\cot\theta = \frac{8}{15} = 0.53$ |

**2)** Find the missing length:

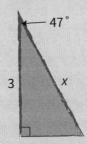

**Answer:**

Identify which side length is known, and which is being solved for in relation to the given angle. With respect to the 47-degree angle, the **h**ypotenuse is the unknown, and the known value is the **a**djacent. The trig function that uses adjacent and hypotenuse is cosine.

| | |
|---|---|
| $\theta = 47$ degrees $a = 3$ $h = x$ | Identify the given parts of the triangle. |
| $\cos 47° = \frac{3}{x}$ $x(\cos 47°) = 3$ $x = \frac{3}{\cos 47°}$ $= \textbf{4.40}$ | Plug these values into the equation for cosine and solve. |

**3)** Find the angle $\theta$ in degrees:

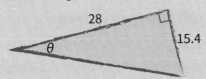

**Answer:**

| | |
|---|---|
| $adjacent = 28$ $opposite = 15.4$ $\theta = ?$ | Identify the given parts of the triangle. |

| | |
|---|---|
| $\tan\theta = \dfrac{opposite}{adjacent}$ | |
| $\tan\theta = \dfrac{15.4}{28}$ | Use the equation for the tangent function to find the angle. |
| $\theta = \tan^{-1}\left(\dfrac{15.4}{28}\right)$ | |
| $\boldsymbol{\theta = 28.81°}$ | |

# The Unit Circle

The **UNIT CIRCLE** is on the coordinate plane, with its center at the origin $(0, 0)$ and a radius of 1. By using triangles within the unit circle (which will all have a hypotenuse of 1), the trigonometric ratios can be extended so that trigonometric functions of *any* angle may be evaluated. In fact, each point $(x, y)$ on the unit circle can be expressed as trig functions of the angle $\theta$: $(x, y) = (\cos\theta, \sin\theta)$.

An angle in **STANDARD POSITION** in the plane has an initial (beginning) ray on the *x*-axis and a terminal (end) ray on the radius of the circle. Positive angles are measured in the counterclockwise direction, and negative angles are measured clockwise from the *x*-axis. One complete circle contains 360°.

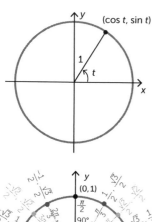

Another way to measure angles is with radians, which involves finding the length of the arc on the circle intercepted by the terminal ray of the angle. Since the circumference of the circle is $C = 2\pi r = 2\pi(1) = 2\pi$, the angle corresponding to one complete circle (360°) has a radian measure of $2\pi$. Other angles can be expressed as fractions of $2\pi$. For example, 90° is $\frac{1}{4}$ of a circle, so its radian measure is $\frac{1}{4}(2\pi) = \frac{\pi}{2}$. A 30° angle would be $\frac{30}{360}(2\pi)$ or $\frac{\pi}{6}$ radians. When the angle intersects the circle such that the arc length is 1, the corresponding angle is 1 radian. The angle in degrees at which this occurs is about 57.3°, so 1 radian $\approx$ 57.3°.

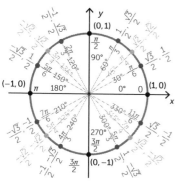

**Figure 2.13. Unit Circle**

Angles can be converted between degrees and radians using these conversion factors:

$$\text{degrees} = \text{radians} \times \frac{180}{\pi} \qquad\qquad \text{radians} = \text{degrees} \times \frac{\pi}{180}$$

Any angle has an infinite number of **COTERMINAL ANGLES** associated with it. These are angles that share the same terminal ray. For example, 390° is coterminal with 30°, because 390° is one complete revolution around the circle plus 30° more, so it lands on the same terminal ray. Another co-terminal angle to this angle would be –330°. To find co-terminal angles in degrees, simply add to or subtract 360° from the angle. In radians, add to or subtract $2\pi$ from the angle.

The unit circle diagram is made up of a number of specific sine and cosine coordinates for angles that are frequently used (often called

A calculator can be put in either radian or degree mode as appropriate for the given problem.

special angles). Tangent on the unit circle is defined as the ratio of sine to cosine, $\tan\theta = \frac{\sin\theta}{\cos\theta}$.

Table 2.8. Special Angle Values in the First Quadrant

| Degrees | 0 | 30 | 45 | 60 | 90 |
|---|---|---|---|---|---|
| Radians | 0 | $\frac{\pi}{6}$ | $\frac{\pi}{4}$ | $\frac{\pi}{3}$ | $\frac{\pi}{2}$ |
| $\sin\theta$ | 0 | $\frac{1}{2}$ | $\frac{\sqrt{2}}{2}$ | $\frac{\sqrt{3}}{2}$ | 1 |
| $\cos\theta$ | 1 | $\frac{\sqrt{3}}{2}$ | $\frac{\sqrt{2}}{2}$ | $\frac{1}{2}$ | 0 |
| $\tan\theta$ | 0 | $\frac{\sqrt{3}}{3}$ | 1 | $\sqrt{3}$ | undefined |

When calculating trig functions of angles in other quadrants, make a sketch of the angle and drop a perpendicular altitude down to the nearest $x$-axis. This forms a triangle. The angle between the $x$-axis and the terminal ray is called the **REFERENCE ANGLE**. It will always be an angle between 0 and $\frac{\pi}{2}$ (or 0 and 90°). If it is one of the special angles, either label the sides of the triangles using the special triangle rules, or use the table above to find the value. In either case, care must be given to the *sign* of the value. As the terminal ray travels into quadrants 2, 3, and 4, the signs of the $x$- and $y$-coordinates are sometimes negative, so the corresponding trig functions will also be negative. This diagram summarizes where each trig function is *positive* (where it is not positive, it is negative!).

To remember in which quadrant each trig function is positive, starting in quad 1, remember ASTC, or All Students Throw Chalk: A = all, S = sine, T = tangent, and C = cosine.

| | |
|---|---|
| Q 2<br>$\sin\theta$ and<br>$\csc\theta$ + | Q 1<br>ALL<br>trig functions<br>+ |
| Q 3<br>$\tan\theta$ and<br>$\cot\theta$ + | Q 4<br>$\cos\theta$ and<br>$\sec\theta$ + |

**Figure 2.14. Trigonometric Signs by Quadrant**

## EXAMPLES

1) Find $\sin\frac{\pi}{2}$.

   **Answer:**

   To make use of a graphing calculator's trigonometric function, make sure it is in radian mode and type in: $\sin\frac{\pi}{2}$, which returns a value of 1. To understand *why* this is true, locate the angle $\frac{\pi}{2}$ on the unit circle. The $\sin \frac{\pi}{2}$ is the $y$-coordinate of the intersection of the terminal ray of angle $\frac{\pi}{2}$ with the unit circle, which is 1 because the ray intersects the circle at point $(0, 1)$.

2) Find $\csc \left( \frac{7\pi}{4} \right)$.

**Answer:**

| | |
|---|---|
| $\csc \dfrac{7\pi}{4} = \dfrac{1}{\sin \frac{7\pi}{4}}$ | Rewrite the expression using the reciprocal identity. |
| $\sin \dfrac{7\pi}{4} = \dfrac{-1}{\sqrt{2}}$ | Find $\frac{7\pi}{4}$ on the unit circle. |
| $\csc \dfrac{7\pi}{4} = \dfrac{1}{\sin \frac{7\pi}{4}} = \dfrac{1}{\frac{-1}{\sqrt{2}}} = -\sqrt{2}$ | Convert sine into cosecant. |

# Conic Sections

**CONIC SECTIONS** refers to the two-dimensional shapes created when a plane intersects a cone. These intersections result in circles, ellipses, hyperbolas, or parabolas depending on the angle at which the plane crosses the cone.

Only hyperbolas have a positive discriminant.

Every conic section equation can be written using the general form for a conic section:

$$Ax^2 + Bxy + Cy^2 + Dx + Ey + F = 0$$

This equation contains two variables ($x$ and $y$) that are both squared. The shape described by the equation can be determined by looking at its coefficients and the value of the conic section discriminant, which is defined as $B^2 - 4AC$.

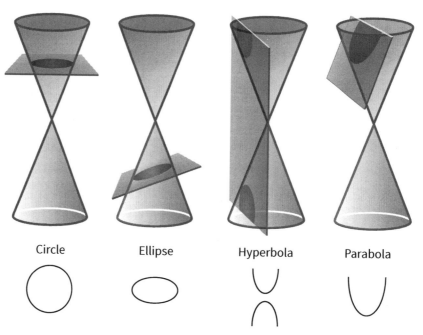

**Figure 2.15. Conic Sections**

Table 2.9. Identifying Conic Sections

| | |
|---|---|
| $B^2 - 4AC < 0$ and $A = C$ | circle |
| $B^2 - 4AC < 0$ and $A \neq C$ | ellipse |
| $B^2 - 4AC > 0$ | hyperbola |
| $B^2 - 4AC < 0$ and $A = 0$ or $C = 0$ | parabola |

## EXAMPLES

**1)** Which conic section is described by the equation $x^2 + y^2 + 6x + 14y = 86$?

**Answer:**

| | |
|---|---|
| $x^2 + y^2 + 6x + 14y = 86$ | |
| $x^2 + y^2 + 6x + 14y - 86 = 0$ | Put the equation in standard form. |
| $A = 1$ <br> $B = 0$ <br> $C = 1$ | Identify the variables needed to solve for the discriminant. |
| $B^2 - 4AC =$ <br> $0^2 - 4(1)(1) =$ <br> $-4$ | Solve for the discriminant. |
| $B^2 - 4AC < 0$ and $A = C$ | **The equation describes a circle.** |

## Circles

The standard form of a circle is written as $(x - h)^2 + (y - k)^2 = r^2$ where $(h, k)$ is the center of the circle and $r$ is its radius.

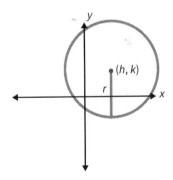

Figure 2.16. Graph of a Circle

## EXAMPLES

**1)** What is the equation for the circle shown on the graph below?

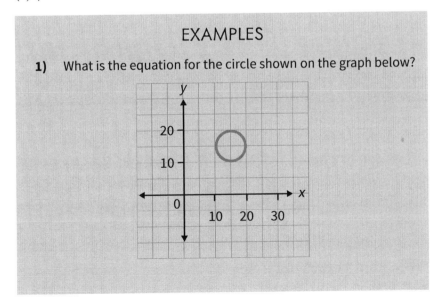

| **Answer:** | |
|---|---|
| $(h,k) = (15,15)$ <br> $r = 5$ | Identify the center and radius of the circle. |
| $(x-h)^2 + (y-k)^2 = r^2$ <br> $(x-15)^2 + (y-15)^2 = 25$ | Plug these values into the standard equation for a circle. |

2) Graph the equation: $-10y + y^2 + x^2 - 38 = -18x$

**Answer:**

| | |
|---|---|
| $-10y + y^2 + x^2 - 38 = -18x$ <br> $x^2 + 18x + y^2 - 10y = 38$ <br> $(x^2 + 18x + 81) + (y^2 - 10y + 25) = 38 + 106$ <br> $(x+9)^2 + (y-5)^2 = 144$ | Convert the equation to standard form by completing the square for each variable. |
| $(h,k) = (-9,5)$ <br> $r = 12$ | Identify the circle's center and radius. |
|  | Graph the circle. |

# Parabolas

PARABOLAS are conic sections formed when only one variable in the general equation is squared. An equation in which the $x$ is squared will open vertically (either up or down). Equations with the $y$ variable squared result in a curve that opens horizontally (either right or left).

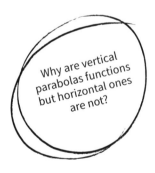

Why are vertical parabolas functions but horizontal ones are not?

Like ellipses and hyperbolas, parabolas have a vertex and a focus, which is a point on the interior of the parabola. The distance from the vertex to the focus is a value called $p$. The AXIS OF SYMMETRY for the parabola will run through both the vertex and focus. Each parabola also has a directrix, which is a line that is a distance of $p$ from the vertex in the opposite direction from the focus. The distance from the focus to any point on the parabola is the same as the distance from that point on the parabola to the directrix.

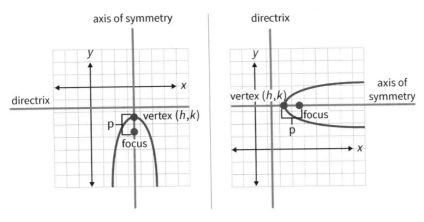

**Figure 2.17. Vertical and Horizontal Parabolas**

Table 2.10. Formulas for Vertical and Horizontal Parabolas

| VERTICAL PARABOLA | HORIZONTAL PARABOLA |
|---|---|
| $(x - h)^2 = 4p(y - k)$ or $y = a(x - h)^2 + k$ | $(y - k)^2 = 4p(x - h)$ or $x = a(y - k)^2 + h$ |
| Vertex: $(h, k)$ | Vertex: $(h, k)$ |
| Focus: $(h, k+p)$ or $(h, k+\frac{1}{4a})$ | Focus: $(h + p, k)$ or $(h + 1/4a, k)$ |
| Axis of Symmetry: $x = h$ | Axis of Symmetry: $y = k$ |
| Directrix: $y = k - p$ or $y = k - \frac{1}{4a}$ | Directrix: $x = h - p$ or $x = h - 1/4a$ |

$$p = \frac{1}{4a}$$

## EXAMPLES

**1)** What is the vertex of a parabola with a directrix of $x = -6$ and a focus of $(2, 1)$?

**Answer:**

The vertex must be equidistant between focus and directrix and have the same $y$ value as the focus, so the vertex is at $(-2, 1)$.

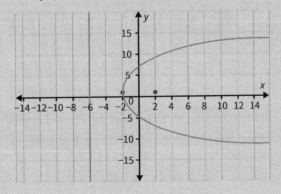

**1)** What is the directrix of the parabola $y = -(x + 3)^2 - 2$?

**Answer:**

$a = -1$

$k = -2$

Identify important values from the equation.

$y = k - \dfrac{1}{4a}$

$y = -2 - \dfrac{1}{4(-1)}$

**$y = -1.75$**

Plug these values into the formula to find the directrix.

three

3

# GEOMETRY

Geometry is the study of shapes, angles, volumes, areas, lines, points, and the relationships among them. It is normally approached as an axiomatic system; that is, a small number of entities are taken for granted as true, and everything else is derived logically from them.

## Equality, Congruence, and Similarity

When discussing shapes in geometry, the term **CONGRUENT** is used to mean that two shapes have the same shape and size (but not necessarily the same orientation or location). This concept is slightly different from equality, which is used in geometry to describe numerical values. For example, if the length of two lines are equal, the two lines themselves are called congruent. Congruence is written using the symbol ≅. On figures, congruent parts are denoted with hash marks.

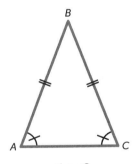

$\angle A \cong \angle C$
$AB \cong BC$

**Figure 3.1. Congruent Parts of a Triangle**

Shapes which are **SIMILAR** have the same shape but the not the same size, meaning their corresponding angles are the same but their lengths are not. For two shapes to be similar, the ratio of their corresponding sides must be a constant (usually written as $k$). Similarity is described using the symbol ~.

## Properties of Shapes

### Basic Definitions

The basic figures from which many other geometric shapes are built are points, lines, and planes. A **POINT** is a location in a plane. It has no size or shape, but is represented by a dot. It is labeled using a capital letter.

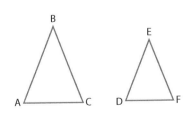

ABC ~ DEF

$$\frac{AB}{DE} = \frac{BC}{EF} = \frac{AC}{DF}$$

**Figure 3.2. Similar Triangles**

A **LINE** is a one-dimensional collection of points that extends infinitely in both directions. At least two points are needed to define a line, and any points that lie on the same line are **COLINEAR**. Lines are represented by two points, such as *A* and *B*, and the line symbol: ($\overleftrightarrow{AB}$). Two lines on the same plane will intersect unless they are **PARALLEL**, meaning they have the same slope. Lines that intersect at a 90 degree angle are **PERPENDICULAR**.

A **LINE SEGMENT** has two endpoints and a finite length. The length of a segment, called the measure of the segment, is the distance from *A* to *B*. A line segment is a subset of a line, and is also denoted with two points, but with a segment symbol: ($\overline{AB}$). The **MIDPOINT** of a line segment is the point at which the segment is divided into two equal parts. A line, segment, or plane that passes through the midpoint of a segment is called a **BISECTOR** of the segment, since it cuts the segment into two equal segments.

A **RAY** has one endpoint and extends indefinitely in one direction. It is defined by its endpoint, followed by any other point on the ray: $\overrightarrow{AB}$. It is important that the first letter represents the endpoint. A ray is sometimes called a half line.

Table 3.1. Basic Geometric Figures

| TERM | DIMENSIONS | GRAPHIC | SYMBOL |
|---|---|---|---|
| point | zero | ● | $\cdot A$ |
| line segment | one | A ——— B | $\overline{AB}$ |
| ray | one | A ——→ B | $\overrightarrow{AB}$ |
| line | one | ←——→ | $\overleftrightarrow{AB}$ |
| plane | two | ▱ | Plane *M* |

A **PLANE** is a flat sheet that extends indefinitely in two directions (like an infinite sheet of paper). A plane is a two-dimensional (2D) figure. A plane can always be defined through any three noncollinear points in three-dimensional (3D) space. A plane is named using any three points that are in the plane (for example, plane *ABC*). Any points lying in the same plane are said to be **COPLANAR**. When two planes intersect, the intersection is a line.

Which points and lines are not contained in plane *M* in the diagram below?

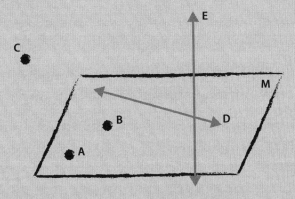

**Answer:**

Points *A* and *B* and line *D* are all on plane *M*. Point *C* is above the plane, and line *E* cuts through the plane and thus does not lie on plane *M*. The point at which line *E* intersects plane *M* is on plane *M* but the line as a whole is not.

# Angles

ANGLES are formed when two rays share a common endpoint. They are named using three letters, with the vertex point in the middle (for example ∠*ABC*, where *B* is the vertex). They can also be labeled with a number or named by their vertex alone (if it is clear to do so). Angles are also classified based on their angle measure. A RIGHT ANGLE has a measure of exactly 90°. ACUTE ANGLES have measures that are less than 90°, and OBTUSE ANGLES have measures that are greater than 90°.

Any two angles that add to make 90° are called COMPLEMENTARY ANGLES. A 30° angle would be complementary to a 60° angle. SUPPLEMENTARY ANGLES add up to 180°. A supplementary angle to a 60° angle would be a 120° angle; likewise, 60° is the SUPPLEMENT of 120°. The complement and supplement of any angle must always be positive. For example, a 140 degree has no complement. Angles that are next to each other and share a common ray are called ADJACENT ANGLES. Angles that are adjacent and supplementary are called a LINEAR PAIR of angles. Their nonshared rays form a line (thus the *linear* pair). Note that angles that are supplementary do not need to be adjacent; their measures simply need to add to 180°.

VERTICAL ANGLES are formed when two lines intersect. Four angles will be formed; the vertex of each angle is at the intersection point of the lines. The vertical angles across from each other will be equal in measure. The angles adjacent to each other will be linear pairs and therefore supplementary.

Angles can be measured in degrees or radian. Use the conversion factor
1 rad = 57.3 degrees
to convert between them.

A ray, line, or segment that divides an angle into two equal angles is called an **ANGLE BISECTOR**.

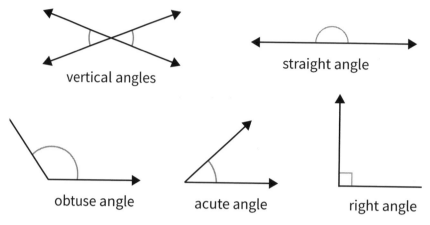

Figure 3.3. Types of Angles

## EXAMPLES

1) How many linear pairs of angles are there in the following figure?

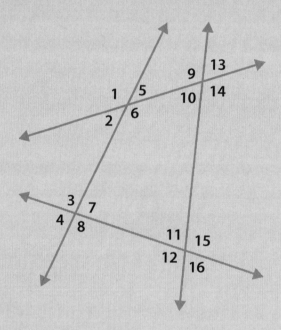

**Answers:**

Any two adjacent angles that are supplementary are linear pairs, so there are 16 linear pairs in the figure (∠1 and ∠5, ∠2 and ∠6, ∠5 and ∠6, ∠2 and ∠1, and so on).

2) If angles *M* and *N* are supplementary and ∠*M* is 30° less than twice ∠*N*, what is the degree measurement of each angle?

**Answer:**

| | |
|---|---|
| $\angle M + \angle N = 180°$ <br><br> $\angle M = 2\angle N - 30°$ | Set up a system of equations. |
| $\angle M + \angle N = 180°$ <br><br> $(2\angle N - 30°) + \angle N = 180°$ <br><br> $3\angle N - 30° = 180°$ <br><br> $3\angle N = 210°$ <br><br> $\angle N = 70°$ | Use substitution to solve for $\angle N$. |
| $\angle M + \angle N = 180°$ <br><br> $\angle M + 70° = 180°$ <br><br> $\angle M = 110°$ | Solve for $\angle M$ using the original equation. |

# Circles

A **CIRCLE** is the set of all the points in a plane that are the same distance from a fixed point called the **CENTER**. The distance from the center to any point on the circle is the **RADIUS** of the circle. The distance around the circle (the perimeter) is called the **CIRCUMFERENCE**.

The ratio of a circle's circumference to its diameter is a constant value called pi ($\pi$), an irrational number which is commonly rounded to 3.14. The formula to find a circle's circumference is $C = 2\pi r$. The formula to find the enclosed area of a circle is $A = \pi r^2$.

Circles have a number of unique parts and properties:

- The **DIAMETER** is the largest measurement across a circle. It passes through the circle's center, extending from one side of the circle to the other. The measure of the diameter is twice the measure of the radius.

- A line that cuts across a circle and touches it twice is called a **SECANT** line. The part of a secant line that lies within a circle is called a **CHORD**. Two chords within a circle are of equal length if they are are the same distance from the center.

- A line that touches a circle or any curve at one point is **TANGENT** to the circle or the curve. These lines are always exterior to the circle. A line tangent to a circle and a radius drawn to the point of tangency meet at a right angle (90°).

- An **ARC** is any portion of a circle between two points on the circle. The **MEASURE** of an arc is in degrees, whereas the **LENGTH OF THE ARC** will be in linear measurement (such as centimeters or inches). A **MINOR ARC** is the small arc between the two points (it measures less than 180°), whereas a **MAJOR ARC** is the large arc between the two points (it measures greater than 180°).

Trying to square a circle means attempting to create a square that has the same area as a circle. Because the area of a circle depends on $\pi$, which is an irrational number, this task is impossible. The phrase is often used to describe trying to do something that can't be done.

- An angle with its vertex at the center of a circle is called a **CENTRAL ANGLE**. For a central angle, the measure of the arc intercepted by the sides of the angle (in degrees) is the same as the measure of the angle.

- A **SECTOR** is the part of a circle *and* its interior that is inside the rays of a central angle (its shape is like a slice of pie).

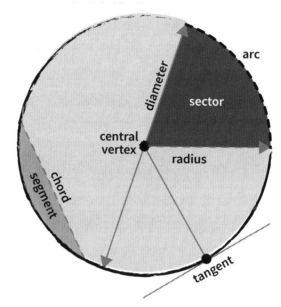

**Figure 3.4. Parts of a Circle**

|         | Area of Sector | Length of an Arc |
|---------|----------------|------------------|
| Degrees | $A = \frac{\theta}{360°} \times \pi r^2$ | $s = \frac{\theta}{360°} \times 2\pi r$ |
| Radians | $A = \frac{1}{2}\pi^2\theta$ | $s = r\theta$ |

- An **INSCRIBED ANGLE** has a vertex on the circle and is formed by two chords that share that vertex point. The angle measure of an inscribed angle is one-half the angle measure of the central angle with the same endpoints on the circle.

- A **CIRCUMSCRIBED ANGLE** has rays tangent to the circle. The angle lies outside of the circle.

- Any angle outside the circle, whether formed by two tangent lines, two secant lines, or a tangent line and a secant line, is equal to half the difference of the intercepted arcs.

- Angles are formed within a circle when two chords intersect in the circle. The measure of the smaller angle formed is half the sum of the two smaller arc measures (in degrees). Likewise, the larger angle is half the sum of the two larger arc measures.

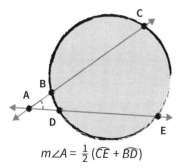

$m\angle A = \frac{1}{2}(\overset{\frown}{CE} + \overset{\frown}{BD})$

**Figure 3.5. Angles Outside a Circle**

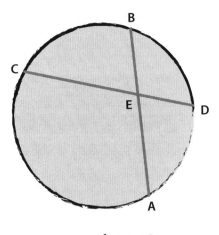

$$m\angle E = \tfrac{1}{2}\left(\widehat{AC} + \widehat{BD}\right)$$

**Figure 3.6. Intersecting Chords**

◆ If a chord intersects a line tangent to the circle, the angle formed by this intersection measures one half the measurement of the intercepted arc (in degrees).

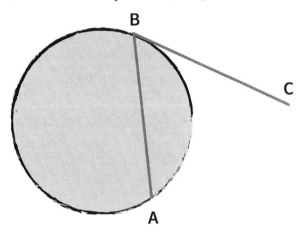

$$m\angle ABC = \tfrac{1}{2}m\widehat{AB}$$

**Figure 3.7. Intersecting Chord and Tangent**

## EXAMPLES

**1)** Find the area of the sector *NHS* of the circle below with center at *H*:

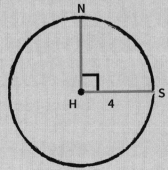

**Answer:**

| | |
|---|---|
| $r = 4$<br><br>$\angle NHS = 90°$ | Identify the important parts of the circle. |
| $A = \dfrac{\theta}{360°} \times \pi r^2$<br><br>$= \dfrac{90}{360} \times \pi(4)^2$ | Plug these values into the formula for the area of a sector. |
| $= \dfrac{1}{4} \times 16\pi$<br><br>$= 4\pi$ | Plug these values into the formula for the area of a sector (continued). |

2) In the circle below with center $O$, the minor arc $ACB$ measures 5 feet. What is the measurement of $m\angle AOB$?

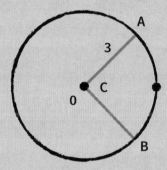

**Answer:**

| | |
|---|---|
| $r = 3$<br><br>length of $\overline{ACB} = 5$ | Identify the important parts of the circle. |
| $s = \dfrac{\theta}{360°} \times 2\pi r$<br><br>$5 = \dfrac{\theta}{360°} \times 2\pi(3)$<br><br>$\dfrac{5}{6\pi} = \dfrac{\theta}{360°}$<br><br>$\theta = 95.5°$<br><br>$\boldsymbol{m\angle AOB = 95.5°}$ | Plug these values into the formula for the length of an arc and solve for $\theta$. |

# Triangles

Much of geometry is concerned with triangles as they are commonly used shapes. A good understanding of triangles allows decomposition of other shapes (specifically polygons) into triangles for study.

Triangles have three sides, and the three interior angles always sum to 180°. The formula for the area of a triangle is $A = \dfrac{1}{2}bh$ or one-half the product of the base and height (or altitude) of the triangle.

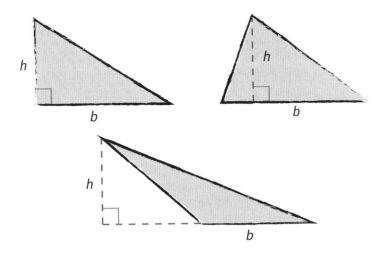

**Figure 3.8. Finding the Base and Height of Triangles**

Some important segments in a triangle include the angle bisector, the altitude, and the median. The ANGLE BISECTOR extends from the side opposite an angle to bisect that angle. The ALTITUDE is the shortest distance from a vertex of the triangle to the line containing the base side opposite that vertex. It is perpendicular to that line and can occur on the outside of the triangle. The MEDIAN extends from an angle to bisect the opposite side.

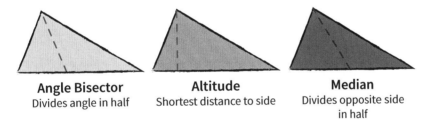

| **Angle Bisector** | **Altitude** | **Median** |
|:---:|:---:|:---:|
| Divides angle in half | Shortest distance to side | Divides opposite side in half |

**Figure 3.9. Important Segments in a Triangle**

Triangles have two "centers." The ORTHOCENTER is formed by the intersection of a triangle's three altitudes. The CENTROID is where a triangle's three medians meet.

Triangles can be classified in two ways: by sides and by angles.

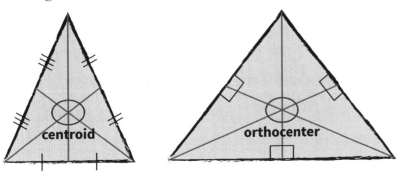

**Figure 3.10. Centroid and Orthocenter of a Triangle**

A SCALENE TRIANGLE has no equal sides or angles. An ISOSCELES TRIANGLE has two equal sides and two equal angles, often called BASE ANGLES. In an EQUILATERAL TRIANGLE, all three sides are equal as are all three angles. Moreover, because the sum of the angles of a triangle is always 180°, each angle of an equilateral triangle must be 60°.

A RIGHT TRIANGLE has one right angle (90°) and two acute angles. An ACUTE TRIANGLE has three acute angles (all angles are less than 90°). An OBTUSE TRIANGLE has one obtuse angle (more than 90°) and two acute angles.

Triangles Based on Sides

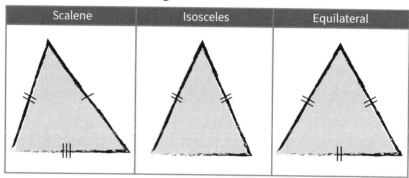

Triangles Based on Angles

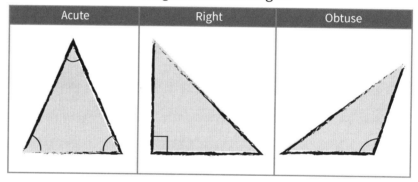

**Figure 3.11. Types of Triangles**

Trigonometric functions can be employed to find missing sides and angles of a triangle.

For any triangle, the side opposite the largest angle will have the longest length, while the side opposite the smallest angle will have the shortest length. The TRIANGLE INEQUALITY THEOREM states that the sum of any two sides of a triangle must be greater than the third side. If this inequality does not hold, then a triangle cannot be formed. A consequence of this theorem is the THIRD-SIDE RULE: if $b$ and $c$ are two sides of a triangle, then the measure of the third side $a$ must be between the sum of the other two sides and the difference of the other two sides: $c - b < a < c + b$.

Solving for missing angles or sides of a triangle is a common type of triangle problem. Often a right triangle will come up on its own or within another triangle. The relationship among a right triangle's sides is known as the PYTHAGOREAN THEOREM: $a^2 + b^2 = c^2$, where $c$ is the hypotenuse and is across from the 90° angle. Right triangles with angle measurements of 90° – 45° – 45° and 90° – 60° – 30° are known as "special" right triangles and have specific relationships between their sides and angles.

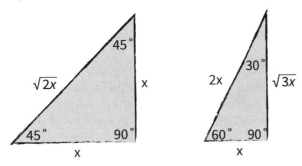

**Figure 3.12. Special Right Triangles**

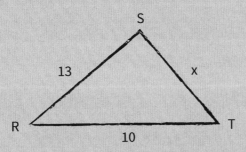
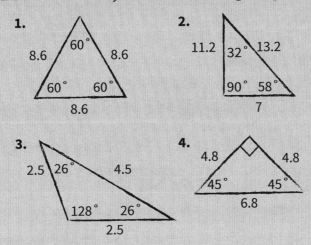

**Answers:**

**Triangle 1 is an equilateral triangle** (all 3 sides are equal, and all 3 angles are equal)

**Triangle 2 is a scalene, right triangle** (all 3 sides are different, and there is a 90° angle)

**Triangle 3 is an obtuse, isosceles triangle** (there are 2 equal sides and, consequently, 2 equal angles)

**Triangle 4 is a right, isosceles triangle** (there are 2 equal sides and a 90° angle)

3) Given the diagram, if $XZ = 100$, $WZ = 80$, and $XU = 70$, then $WY = ?$

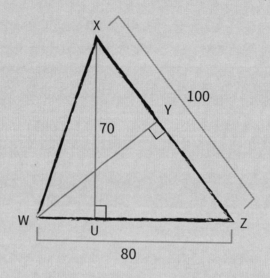

**Answer:**

$WZ = b_1 = 80$

$XU = h_1 = 70$

$XZ = b_2 = 100$

$WY = h_2 = ?$

| | |
|---|---|
| $A = \frac{1}{2}bh$ <br> $A_1 = \frac{1}{2}(80)(70) = 2800$ <br> $A_2 = \frac{1}{2}(100)(h_2)$ | The given values can be used to write two equation for the area of $\triangle WXZ$ with two sets of bases and heights. |
| $2800 = \frac{1}{2}(100)(h_2)$ <br> $h_2 = 56$ <br> **$WY = 56$** | Set the two equations equal to each other and solve for $WY$. |

# Quadrilaterals

All closed, four-sided shapes are **QUADRILATERALS**. The sum of all internal angles in a quadrilateral is always 360°. (Think of drawing a diagonal to create two triangles. Since each triangle contains 180°, two triangles, and therefore the quadrilateral, must contain 360°.) The **AREA OF ANY QUADRILATERAL** is $A = bh$, where $b$ is the base and $h$ is the height (or altitude).

A **PARALLELOGRAM** is a quadrilateral with two pairs of parallel sides. A rectangle is a parallelogram with two pairs of equal sides and four right angles. A **KITE** also has two pairs of equal sides, but its equal sides are consecutive. Both a **SQUARE** and a **RHOMBUS** have four equal sides. A square has four right angles, while a rhombus has a pair of acute opposite angles and a pair of obtuse opposite angles. A **TRAPEZOID** has exactly one pair of parallel sides.

All squares are rectangles and all rectangles are parallelograms; however, not all parallelograms are rectangles and not all rectangles are squares.

Table 3.2. Properties of Parallelograms

| TERM | SHAPE | PROPERTIES |
|---|---|---|
| Parallelogram | | Opposite sides are parallel. Consecutive angles are supplementary. Opposite angles are equal. Opposite sides are equal. Diagonals bisect each other. |
| Rectangle | | All parallelogram properties hold. Diagonals are congruent *and* bisect each other. All angles are right angles. |
| Square | | All rectangle properties hold. All four sides are equal. Diagonals bisect angles. Diagonals intersect at right angles and bisect each other. |
| Kite | | One pair of opposite angles is equal. Two pairs of consecutive sides are equal. Diagonals meet at right angles. |
| Rhombus | | All four sides are equal. Diagonals bisect angles. Diagonals intersect at right angles and bisect each other. |
| Trapezoid | | One pair of sides is parallel. Bases have different lengths. Isosceles trapezoids have a pair of equal sides (and base angles). |

## EXAMPLES

1) In parallelogram *ABCD*, the measure of angle *m* is is $m° = 260°$. What is the measure of $n°$?

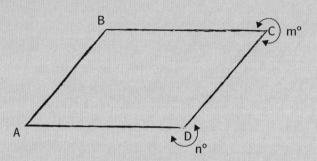

**Answers:**

| | |
|---|---|
| $260° + m\angle C = 360°$ <br> $m\angle C = 100°$ | Find $\angle C$ using the fact that the sum of $\angle C$ and *m* is 360°. |
| $m\angle C + m\angle D = 180°$ <br> $100° + m\angle D = 180°$ <br> $m\angle D = 80°$ | Solve for $\angle D$ using the fact that consecutive interior angles in a quadrilateral are supplementary. |
| $m\angle D + n = 360°$ <br> **$n = 280°$** | Solve for *n* by subtracting $m\angle D$ from 360°. |

2) A rectangular section of a football field has dimensions of *x* and *y* and an area of 1000 square feet. Three additional lines drawn vertically divide the section into four smaller rectangular areas as seen in the diagram below. If all the lines shown need to be painted, calculate the total number of linear feet, in terms of *x*, to be painted.

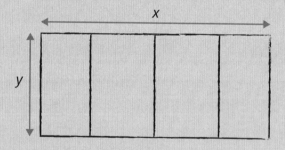

**Answer:**

| | |
|---|---|
| $A = 1000 = xy$ <br> $L = 2x + 5y$ | Find equations for the area of the field and length of the lines to be painted (*L*) in terms of *x* and *y*. |
| $y = \frac{1000}{x}$ <br> $L = 2x + 5y$ <br> $L = 2x + 5\left(\frac{1000}{x}\right)$ <br> **$L = 2x + \frac{5000}{x}$** | Substitute to find *L* in terms of *x*. |

# Polygons

Any closed shape made up of three or more line segments is a polygon. In addition to triangles and quadrilaterals, HEXAGONS and OCTAGONS are two common polygons.

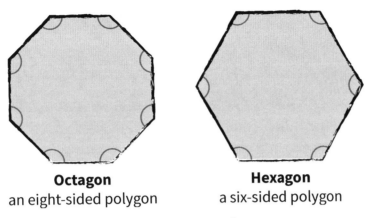

**Octagon**
an eight-sided polygon

**Hexagon**
a six-sided polygon

**Figure 3.13. Common Polygons**

The two polygons depicted above are REGULAR POLYGONS, meaning that they are equilateral (all sides having equal lengths) and equiangular (all angles having equal measurements). Angles inside a polygon are INTERIOR ANGLES, whereas those formed by one side of the polygon and a line extending outside the polygon are EXTERIOR ANGLES:

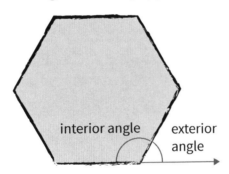

interior angle    exterior angle

**Figure 3.14 Interior and Exterior Angles**

The sum of the all the exterior angles of a polygon is always 360°. Dividing 360° by the number of a polygon's sides finds the measure of the polygon's exterior angles.

To determine the sum of a polygon's interior angles in a regular polygon, choose one vertex and draw diagonals from that vertex to each of the other vertices, decomposing the polygon into multiple triangles. For example, an octagon has six triangles within it, and therefore the sum of the interior angles is 6 × 180° = 1080°. In general, the formula for finding the sum of the angles in a polygon is *sum of angles* = $(n - 2)$ × 180°, where $n$ is the number of sides of the polygon.

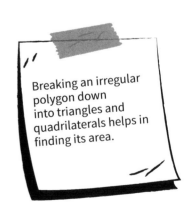

Breaking an irregular polygon down into triangles and quadrilaterals helps in finding its area.

To find the measure of a single interior angle, simply divide the sum of the interior angles by the number of angles (which is the same as the number of sides). So, in the octagon example, each angle is $\frac{1080}{8} = 135°$.

In general, the formula to find the measure of a regular polygon's interior angles is: *interior angle* $= \frac{(n-2)}{n} \times 180°$ where *n* is the number of sides of the polygon.

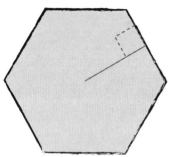

**Figure 3.15. Apothem in a Hexagon**

To find the area of a polygon, it is helpful to know the perimeter of the polygon (*p*), and the **APOTHEM** (*a*). The apothem is the shortest (perpendicular) distance from the polygon's center to one of the sides of the polygon. The formula for the area is: *area* $= \frac{ap}{2}$.

Finally, there is no universal way to find the perimeter of a polygon (when the side length is not given). Often, breaking the polygon down into triangles and adding the base of each triangle all the way around the polygon is the easiest way to calculate the perimeter.

## EXAMPLES

1) What is the measure of an exterior angle and an interior angle of a regular 400-gon?

**Answer:**

The sum of the exterior angles is 360°. Dividing this sum by 400 gives $\frac{360°}{400} = \mathbf{0.9°}$. Since an interior angle is supplementary to an exterior angle, all the interior angles have measure 180 − 0.9 = **179.1°**. Alternately, using the formula for calculating the interior angle gives the same result:

*interior angle* $= \frac{400-2}{400} \times 180° = 179.1°$

2) The circle and hexagon below both share center point *T*. The hexagon is entirely inscribed in the circle. The circle's radius is 5. What is the area of the shaded area?

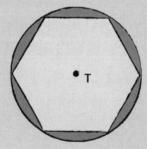

**Answer:**

$A_c = \pi r^2$

$= \pi(5)^2$

$= 25\pi$

The area of the shaded region will be the area of the circle minus the area of the hexagon. Use the radius to find the area of the circle.

| | |
|---|---|
| $a = 2.5\sqrt{3}$ <br><br> $A_H = \dfrac{ap}{2}$ <br><br> $= \dfrac{(2.5\sqrt{3})(30)}{2}$ <br><br> $= 64.95$ | To find the area of the hexagon, draw a right triangle from the vertex, and use special right triangles to find the hexagon's apothem. Then, use the apothem to calculate the area. |
| $= A_c - A_H$ <br> $= 25\pi - 2.5\sqrt{3}$ <br> $\approx \textbf{13.59}$ | Subtract the area of the hexagon from the circle to find the area of the shaded region. |

# Three-Dimensional Shapes

## Properties of Three-Dimensional Shapes

THREE-DIMENSIONAL SHAPES have depth in addition to width and length. VOLUME is expressed as the number of cubic units any solid can hold—that is, what it takes to fill it up. SURFACE AREA is the sum of the areas of the two-dimensional figures that are found on its surface. Some three-dimensional shapes also have a unique property called a slant height ($\ell$), which is the distance from the base to the apex along a lateral face.

Table 3.3. Three-Dimensional Shapes and Formulas

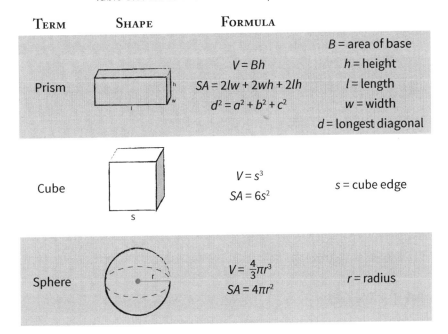

| TERM | SHAPE | FORMULA | |
|---|---|---|---|
| Prism | | $V = Bh$ <br> $SA = 2lw + 2wh + 2lh$ <br> $d^2 = a^2 + b^2 + c^2$ | $B$ = area of base <br> $h$ = height <br> $l$ = length <br> $w$ = width <br> $d$ = longest diagonal |
| Cube | | $V = s^3$ <br> $SA = 6s^2$ | $s$ = cube edge |
| Sphere | | $V = \frac{4}{3}\pi r^3$ <br> $SA = 4\pi r^2$ | $r$ = radius |

Table 3.3. Three-Dimensional Shapes and Formulas (continued)

| TERM | SHAPE | FORMULA | |
|---|---|---|---|
| Cylinder | | $V = Bh = \pi r^2 h$ <br> $SA = 2\pi r^2 + 2\pi rh$ | $B$ = area of base <br> $h$ = height <br> $r$ = radius |
| Cone | | $V = \frac{1}{3}\pi r^2 h$ <br> $SA = \pi r^2 + \pi rl$ | $r$ = radius <br> $h$ = height <br> $l$ = slant height |
| Pyramid | | $V = \frac{1}{3}Bh$ <br> $SA = B + \frac{1}{2}(p)l$ | $B$ = area of base <br> $h$ = height <br> $p$ = perimeter <br> $l$ = slant height |

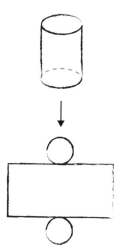

**Figure 3.16. Net of a Cylinder**

Finding the surface area of a three-dimensional solid can be made easier by using a NET. This two-dimensional "flattened" version of a three-dimensional shape shows the component parts that comprise the surface of the solid.

## EXAMPLES

1) A sphere has a radius $z$. If that radius is increased by $t$, by how much is the surface area increased? Write the answer in terms of $z$ and $t$.

**Answer:**

| | |
|---|---|
| $SA_1 = 4\pi z^2$ | Write the equation for the area of the original sphere. |
| $SA_2 = 4\pi(z + t)^2$ <br> $= 4\pi(z^2 + 2zt + t^2)$ <br> $= 4\pi z^2 + 8\pi zt + 4\pi t^2$ | Write the equation for the area of the new sphere. |
| $A_2 - A_1 = 4\pi z^2 + 8\pi zt + 4\pi t^2 - 4\pi z^2$ <br> $\mathbf{= 4\pi t^2 + 8\pi zt}$ | To find the difference between the two, subtract the original from the increased surface area: |

2) A cube with volume 27 cubic meters is inscribed within a sphere such that all of the cube's vertices touch the sphere. What is the length of the sphere's radius?

# Congruence and Similarity in Three-Dimensional Shapes

Three-dimensional shapes may also be congruent if they are the same size and shape, or similar if their corresponding parts are proportional. For example, a pair of cones is similar if the ratios of the cones' radii and heights are proportional. For rectangular prisms, all three dimensions must be proportional for the prisms to be similar. If two shapes are similar, their corresponding areas and volumes will also be proportional. If the constant of proportionality of the linear measurements of a 3D shape is $k$, the constant of proportionality between the areas will be $k^2$, and the constant of proportionality between the volumes will be $k^3$.

All spheres are similar as a dilation of the radius of a sphere will make it equivalent to any other sphere.

## EXAMPLES

1) A square-based pyramid has a height of 10 cm. If the length of the side of the square is 6 cm, what is the surface area of the pyramid?

   **Answer:**

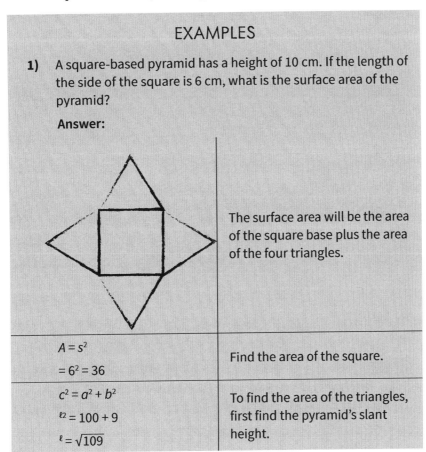

| | |
|---|---|
| | The surface area will be the area of the square base plus the area of the four triangles. |
| $A = s^2$ $= 6^2 = 36$ | Find the area of the square. |
| $c^2 = a^2 + b^2$ $\ell^2 = 100 + 9$ $\ell = \sqrt{109}$ | To find the area of the triangles, first find the pyramid's slant height. |

| | |
|---|---|
| $A = \frac{1}{2}bh$ $A = \frac{1}{2}(6)(\sqrt{109})$ $A = 3\sqrt{109}$ | Find the area of the triangle face using the slant height as the height of the triangle face. |
| $SA = 36 + 4(3\sqrt{109})$ $\approx \textbf{161.3 cm}^2$ | Add the area of the square base and the four triangles to find the total surface area. |

**2)** Given that two cones are similar and one cone's radius is three times longer than the other's radius, what is the volume of the smaller cone if the larger cone has a volume of $81\pi$ cubic inches and a height of 3 inches?

**Answer:**

| | |
|---|---|
| $V_1 = 81\pi$ $h_1 = 3$ | Identify the given variables. |
| $V_1 = \frac{1}{3}\pi r_1^2 h_1$ $81\pi = \frac{1}{3}\pi(r_1)(3)$ $r_1 = 9$ | Find the radius of the larger cone with the given information. |
| $r_2 = \frac{1}{3}r_1$ $r_2 = \frac{1}{3}(9)$ $r_2 = 3$ $h_2 = \frac{1}{3}h_1$ $h_2 = \frac{1}{3}(3)$ $h_2 = 1$ | Use the given scale factor to find the second cone's radius and height. |
| $V_2 = \frac{1}{3}\pi r_2^2 h_2$ $V_2 = \frac{1}{3}\pi(3)^2(1)$ $\textbf{V}_2 = \textbf{3}\boldsymbol{\pi}$ | Find the area of the smaller cone. |

# Transformations of Geometric Figures

## Basic Transformations

Transformation follow the order of operations. For example, to transform the function $y = a[f(x - h)] + k$:
1. Translate the function right/left $h$ units.
2. Dilate the function by the scale factor $a$.
3. Reflect the graph if $a < 0$.
4. Translate the function up/down $k$ units.

Geometric figures are often drawn in the coordinate $xy$-plane, with the vertices or centers of the figures indicated by ordered pairs. These shapes can then be manipulated by performing TRANSFORMATIONS, which alter the size or shape of the figure using mathematical operations. The original shape is called the PRE-IMAGE, and the shape after a transformation is applied is called the IMAGE.

A **TRANSLATION** transforms a shape by moving it right or left, or up or down. Translations are sometimes called slides. After this transformation, the image is identical in size and shape to the pre-image. In other words, the image is **CONGRUENT**, or identical in size, to the pre-image. All corresponding pairs of angles are congruent, and all corresponding side lengths are congruent.

Translations are often in brackets: $(x, y)$. The first number represents the change in the $x$ direction (left/right), while the second number shows the change in the $y$ direction (up/down).

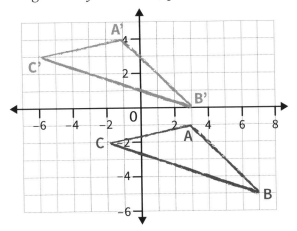

The translation moved triangle ABC left 4 units and up 6 units to produce triangle A'B'C'.

**Figure 3.17. Translation**

Similarly, rotations and reflections preserve the size and shape of the figure, so congruency is preserved. A **ROTATION** takes a pre-image and rotates it about a fixed point (often the origin) in the plane. Although the position or orientation of the shape changes, the angles and side lengths remain the same.

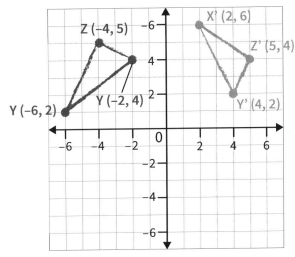

The triangle XYZ is rotated 90 in the clockwise direction about the origin (0, 0).

**Figure 3.18. Rotation**

A REFLECTION takes each point in the pre-image and flips it over a point or line in the plane (often the $x$- or $y$-axis, but not necessarily). The image is congruent to the pre-image. When a figure is flipped across the $y$-axis, the signs of all $x$-coordinates will change. The $y$-coordinates change sign when a figure is reflected across the $x$-axis.

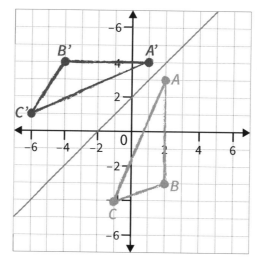

The triangle ABC is reflected over the line to produce the triangle A'B'C'.

**Figure 3.19. Reflection**

---

## EXAMPLE

1) If quadrilateral *ABCD* has vertices *A* (−6, 4), *B* (−6, 8), *C* (2, 8), and *D* (4, −4), what are the new vertices if *ABCD* is translated 2 units down and 3 units right?

**Answer:**

Translating two units down decreases each *y*-value by 2, and moving 3 units to the right increases the *x*-value by 3. The new vertices are *A* (−3, 2), *B* (−3, 6), *C* (5, 6), and *D* (7, −6).

---

# Dilations and Similarity

A DILATION increases (or decreases) the size of a figure by some SCALE FACTOR. Each coordinate of the points that make up the figure is multiplied by the same factor. If the factor is greater than 1, multiplying all the factors enlarges the shape; if the factor is less than 1 (but greater than 0), the shape is reduced in size.

In addition to the scale factor, a dilation needs a CENTER OF DILATION, which is a fixed point in the plane about which the points are multiplied. Usually, but not always, the center of dilation is the origin (0, 0). For dilations about the origin, the image coordinates are calculated by multiplying each coordinate by the scale factor **k**. Thus, point **(x, y) → (kx, ky)**. Although dilations do not result in congruent figures, the orientation of the figure is preserved; consequently, corresponding line segments will be parallel.

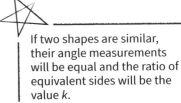

If two shapes are similar, their angle measurements will be equal and the ratio of equivalent sides will be the value *k*.

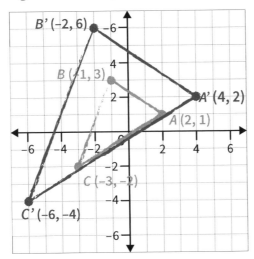

The triangle ABC is dilated by the scale factor 2 to produce triangle A'B'C'.

**Figure 3.20. Dilation**

Importantly, dilations do NOT create images that are congruent to the original because the size of each dimension is increased or decreased (the only exception being if the scale factor is exactly 1). However, the shape of the figure is maintained. The corresponding angle measures will be congruent, but the corresponding side lengths will be *proportional*. In other words, the image and pre-image will be SIMILAR shapes (described with the symbol ~).

---

### EXAMPLE

If quadrilateral *ABCD* has vertices *A* (–6, 4), *B* (–6, 8), *C* (2, 8), and *D* (4, –4), what are the new vertices if *ABCD* is increased by a factor of 5 about the origin?

**Answer:**

Multiply each point by the scale factor of 5 to find the new vertices: *A* (–30, 20), *B* (–30, 40), *C* (10, 40), **and** *D* (20, –20).

---

## Transforming Coordinates

Transformations in a plane can actually be thought of as functions. An input pair of coordinates, when acted upon by a transformation, results in a pair of output coordinates. Each point is moved to a unique new point (a one-to-one correspondence).

Table 3.4. How Coordinates Change for Transformations in a Plane

| TYPE OF TRANSFORMATION | COORDINATE CHANGES |
|---|---|
| Translation right $m$ units and up $n$ units | $(x, y) \rightarrow (x + m, y + n)$ |
| Rotations about the origin in positive (counterclockwise) direction | |
| **Rotation 90°** | $(x, y) \rightarrow (-y, x)$ |
| **Rotation 180°** | $(x, y) \rightarrow (-x, -y)$ |
| **Rotation 270°** | $(x, y) \rightarrow (y, -x)$ |
| Reflections about the | |
| **x-axis** | $(x, y) \rightarrow (x, -y)$ |
| **y-axis** | $(x, y) \rightarrow (-x, y)$ |
| line **y = x** | $(x, y) \rightarrow (y, x)$ |
| Dilations about the origin by a factor of $k$ **0 < k < 1 → size reduced** **k > 1 → size enlarged** | $(x, y) \rightarrow (kx, ky)$ |

## EXAMPLES

1) Triangle *ABC* with coordinates $(2, 8)$, $(10, 2)$, and $(6, 8)$ is transformed in the plane as shown in the diagram. What transformations result in the image triangle *A'B'C'*?

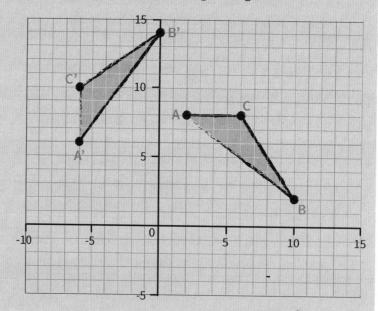

**Answer:**

Since the orientation of the triangle is different from the original, it must have been rotated. A counterclockwise rotation of 90° about the point *A* $(2, 8)$ results in a triangle with the same orientation. Then the triangle must be translated to move it to the image location. Pick one point, say *A*, and determine the translation necessary to move it to point A'. In this case, each point on the pre-image must be translated 8 units left and 2 units down, or (−8, −2). (Note that this is one of many possible answers.)

2) If quadrilateral *ABCD* has vertices *A* (−6, 4), *B* (−6, 8), *C* (2, 8), and *D* (4, −4), what are the new vertices if *ABCD* is rotated 270° and then reflected across the *x*-axis?

**Answer:**

When a figure is rotated 270°, the coordinates change: $(a, b) \rightarrow (b, -a)$. After the rotation, the new coordinates are (4, 6), (8, 6), (8, −2), and (−4, −4). Reflecting across the *x*-axis requires that every *y*-value is multiplied by −1 to arrive at the completely transformed quadrilateral with vertices of (4, −6), (8, −6), (8, 2), and (−4, 4).

# four

# STATISTICS

Statistics is the study of DATA, which are simply sets of qualitative and quantitative values. These values are often the result of observations or measurements collected as part of experiments or surveys. The sections below discuss how to organize, analyze, and present data in a variety of ways.

## Describing Sets of Data

### Measures of Central Tendency

Measures of central tendency help identify the center, or most typical, value within a data set. There are three such central tendencies that describe the "center" of the data in different ways. The MEAN is the arithmetic average and is found by dividing the sum of all measurements by the number of measurements. The mean of a population is written as $\mu$ and the mean of a sample is written as $\overline{x}$.

$$\text{population mean} = \mu = \frac{x_1 + x_2 + \dots x_N}{N} = \frac{\Sigma x}{N}$$

$$\text{sample mean} = \overline{x} = \frac{x_1 + x_2 + \dots x_n}{n} = \frac{\Sigma x}{n}$$

The data points are represented by $x$'s with subscripts; the sum is denoted using the Greek letter sigma ($\Sigma$); $N$ is the number of data points in the entire population; and $n$ is the number of data points in a sample set.

The MEDIAN divides the measurements into two equal halves. The median is the measurement right in the middle of an odd set of measurements or the average of the two middle numbers in an even data set. When calculating the median, it is important to order the data values from least to greatest before attempting to locate the middle value. The MODE is simply the measurement that occurs most often. There can

When the same value is added to each term in a set, the mean increases by that value and the standard deviation is unchanged. When each term in a set is multiplied by the same value, both the mean and standard deviation will also be multiplied by that value.

be many modes in a data set, or no mode. Since measures of central tendency describe a *center* of the data, all three of these measures will be between the lowest and highest data values (inclusive).

Unusually large or small values, called OUTLIERS, will affect the mean of a sample more than the mode. If there is a high outlier, the mean will be greater than the median; if there is a low outlier, the mean will be lower than the median. When outliers are present, the median is a better measure of the data's center than the mean because the median will be closer to the terms in the data set.

## EXAMPLES

**1)** What is the mean of the following data set? {1000, 0.1, 10, 1}

**Answer:**

Use the equation to find the mean of a sample:

$$\frac{1000 + 0.1 + 10 + 1}{4} = \mathbf{252.78}$$

**2)** What is the median of the following data set? {1000, 10, 1, 0.1}

**Answer:**

Since there are an even number of data points in the set, the median will be the mean of the two middle numbers. Order the numbers from least to greatest: 0.1, 1, 10, and 1000. The two middle numbers are 1 and 10, and their mean is:

$$\frac{1 + 10}{2} = \mathbf{5.5}$$

**3)** Josey has an average of 81 on four equally weighted tests she has taken in her statistics class. She wants to determine what grade she must receive on her fifth test so that her mean is 83, which will give her a B in the course, but she does not remember her other scores. What grade must she receive on her fifth test?

**Answer:**

Even though Josey does not know her test scores, she knows her average. Therefore it can be assumed that each test score was 81, since four scores of 81 would average to 81. To find the score, $x$, that she needs use the equation for the mean of a sample:

$$\frac{4(81) + x}{5} = 83$$

$$324 + x = 415$$

$$x = \mathbf{91}$$

## Measures of Variation

The values in a data set can be very close together (close to the mean), or very spread out. This is called the SPREAD or DISPERSION of the data. There are a few MEASURES OF VARIATION (or MEASURES OF DIS-

PERSION) that quantify the spread within a data set. **RANGE** is the difference between the largest and smallest data points in a set:

*R = largest data point – smallest data point*

Notice range depends on only two data points (the two extremes). Sometimes these data points are outliers; regardless, for a large data set, relying on only two data points is not an exact tool.

The understanding of the data set can be improved by calculating **QUARTILES**. To calculate quartiles, first arrange the data in ascending order and find the set's median (also called quartile 2 or Q2). Then find the median of the lower half of the data, called quartile 1 (Q1), and the median of the upper half of the data, called quartile 3 (Q3). These three points divide the data into four equal groups of data (thus the word *quartile*). Each quartile contains 25% of the data.

**INTERQUARTILE RANGE (IQR)** provides a more reliable range that is not as affected by extremes. IQR is the difference between the third quartile data point and the first quartile data point and gives the spread of the middle 50% of the data:

$$IQR = Q_3 - Q_1$$

A measure of variation that depends on the mean is **STANDARD DEVIATION**, which uses every data point in a set and calculates the average distance of each data point from the mean of the data. Standard deviation can be computed for an entire population (written $\sigma$) or for a sample of a population (written $s$):

$$\sigma = \sqrt{\frac{\Sigma(x_i - \mu)^2}{N}} \qquad s = \sqrt{\frac{\Sigma(x_i - \bar{x})^2}{n - 1}}$$

Standard deviation and variance are also affected by extreme values. Though much simpler to calculate, interquartile range is the more accurate depiction of how the data is scattered when there are outlier values.

Thus, to calculate standard deviation, the difference between the mean and each data point is calculated. Each of these differences is squared (so that each is positive). The average of the squared values is computed by summing the squares and dividing by $N$ or $(n - 1)$. Then the square root is taken, to "undo" the previous squaring.

The **VARIANCE** of a data set is simply the square of the standard variation:

$$V = \sigma^2 = \frac{1}{N} \sum_{i=1}^{N} (x_i - \mu)^2$$

Variance measures how narrowly or widely the data points are distributed. A variance of zero means every data point is the same; a large variance means the data is widely spread out.

## EXAMPLES

**1)** What are the range and interquartile range of the following set? {3, 9, 49, 64, 81, 100, 121, 144, 169}

**Answer:**

| | |
|---|---|
| $R =$ largest point − smallest point<br><br>$= 169 - 3$<br><br>$= \mathbf{166}$ | Use the equation for range. |
| 3<br><br>9<br><br>→ Q1 $= \dfrac{49 + 9}{2} = 29$<br><br>49<br><br>64<br><br>81 → Q2<br><br>100<br><br>121<br><br>→ Q3 $= \dfrac{121 + 144}{2} = 132.5$<br><br>144<br><br>169 | Place the terms in numerical order and identify Q1, Q2, and Q3. |
| IQR $=$ Q3 − Q1<br><br>$= 132.5 - 29$<br><br>$= \mathbf{103.5}$ | Find the IQR by subtracting Q1 from Q3. |

2) In a group of 7 people, 1 person has no children, 2 people have 1 child, 2 people have 2 children, 1 person has 5 children, and 1 person has 17 children. To the nearest hundredth of a child, what is the standard deviation in this group?

**Answer:**

| | |
|---|---|
| $\{0, 1, 1, 2, 2, 5, 17\}$ | Create a data set out of this scenario. |
| $\mu = \dfrac{x_1 + x_2 + \ldots x_N}{N} = \dfrac{\Sigma x}{N}$<br><br>$\mu = \dfrac{0 + 1 + 1 + 2 + 2 + 5 + 17}{7} = 4$ | Calculate the population mean. |
| $(0 - 4)^2 = (-4)^2 = 16$<br><br>$(1 - 4)^2 = (-3)^2 = 9$<br><br>$(1 - 4)^2 = (-3)^2 = 9$<br><br>$(2 - 4)^2 = (-2)^2 = 4$<br><br>$(2 - 4)^2 = (-2)^2 = 4$<br><br>$(5 - 4)^2 = (1)^2 = 1$<br><br>$(17 - 4)^2 = (13)^2 = 169$ | Find the square of the difference of each term and the mean $(x_i - \mu)^2$. |
| $\sigma = \sqrt{\dfrac{\Sigma(x_i - \mu)^2}{N}}$<br><br>$\sigma = \sqrt{\dfrac{212}{7}} = \sqrt{30.28} = \mathbf{5.50}$ | Plug the sum ($\Sigma$) of these squares, 212, into the standard deviation formula. |

# Box Plots

A box plot depicts the median and quartiles along a scaled number line. It is meant to summarize the data in a visual manner and emphasize central trends while decreasing the pull of outlier data. To construct a box plot:

1. Create a number line that begins at the lowest data point and terminates at the highest data point.

2. Find the quartiles of the data. Create a horizontal rectangle (the "box") whose left border is $Q_1$ and right border is $Q_3$.

3. Draw a vertical line within the box to mark the median.

4. Draw a horizontal line going from the left edge of the box to the smallest data value.

5. Draw a horizontal line going from the right edge of the box to the largest data value.

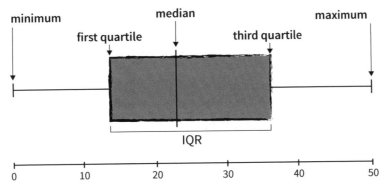

**Figure 4.1. Box Plot**

When reading a box plot, the following stands out:

◆ Reading from left to right: the horizontal line (whisker) shows the spread of the first quarter; the box's left compartment shows the spread of the second quarter; the box's right compartment shows the spread of the third quarter; and the right horizontal line shows the spread of the fourth quarter.

◆ The length of the box is the IQR, or the middle 50% of the data.

◆ Each of the four pieces (the whiskers and two pieces in the box) represent 25% of the data.

◆ The horizontal lines show by their length whether the data higher or lower than the middle 50% is prominent.

Box plots are also known as box-and-whisker plots, because if they are drawn correctly the two horizontal lines look like whiskers.

A recent survey asked 8 people how many pairs of shoes they wear per week. Their answers are in the following data set: {1, 3, 5, 5, 7, 8, 12}. Construct a box plot from this data.

**Answer:**

Create a number line that begins at 1 and ends at 12. $Q_1$ is 3, the median ($Q_2$) is 5, and $Q_3$ is 8. A rectangle must be drawn whose length is 5 and that borders on $Q_1$ and $Q_3$. Mark the median of 5 within the rectangle. Draw a horizontal line going left to 1. Draw a horizontal line going right to 12.

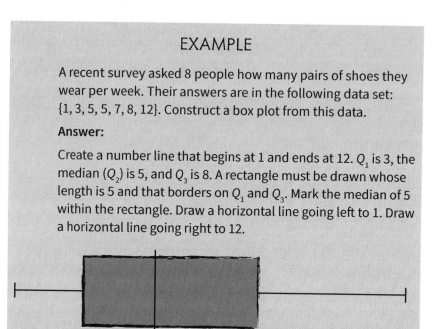

# Graphs, Charts, and Tables

## Pie Charts

A pie chart simply states the proportion of each category within the whole. To construct a pie chart, the categories of a data set must be determined. The frequency of each category must be found and that frequency converted to a percent of the total. To draw the pie chart, determine the angle of each slice by multiplying the percentage by 360°.

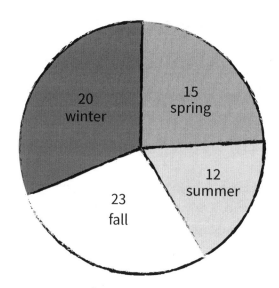

**Figure 4.2. Pie Chart**

A firm is screening applicants for a job by education-level attainment. There are 125 individuals in the pool: 5 have a doctorate, 20 have a master's degree, 40 have a bachelor's degree, 30 have an associate degree, and 30 have a high school degree. Construct a pie chart showing the highest level of education attained by the applicants.

**Answer:**

Create a frequency table to find the percentages and angle measurement for each category.

| Category | Frequency | Percent | Angle Measure |
|----------|-----------|---------|---------------|
| High School | 30 | 24% | 86.4 |
| Associate | 30 | 24% | 86.4 |
| Bachelor's | 40 | 32% | 115.2 |
| Master's | 20 | 16% | 57.6 |
| Doctorate | 5 | 4% | 14.4 |

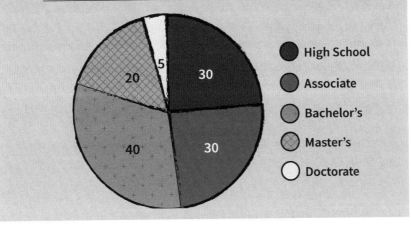

# Scatter Plots

A scatter plot is displayed in the first quadrant of the *xy*-plane where all numbers are positive. Data points are plotted as ordered pairs, with one variable along the horizontal axis and the other along the vertical axis. Scatter plots can show if there is a correlation between two variables. There is a **POSITIVE CORRELATION** (expressed as a positive slope) if increasing one variable appears to result in an increase in the other variable. A **NEGATIVE CORRELATION** (expressed as a negative slope) occurs when an increase in one variable causes a decrease in the other. If the scatter plot shows no discernible pattern, then there is no correlation (a zero, mixed, or indiscernible slope).

Calculators or other software can be used to find the linear regression equation, which describes the general shape of the data. Graphing this equation produces the regression line, or line of best fit. The equation's **correlation coefficient** (*r*) can be used to determine how closely the equation fits the data. The value of $r$ is between –1 and 1. The closer $r$ is to 1 (if the line has a positive slope) or –1 (if the line has a negative slope), the better the regression line fits the data. The closer the $r$ value is to 0, the weaker the correlation between the line and the data. Generally, if the absolute value of the correlation coefficient is 0.8 or higher, then it is considered to be a strong correlation, while an |$r$| value of less than 0.5 is considered a weak correlation.

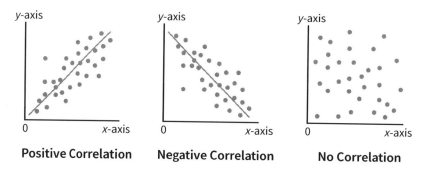

Figure 4.3. Scatter Plots and Correlation

To determine which curve is the "best fit" for a set of data, RESIDUALS are calculated. The calculator automatically calculates and saves these values to a list called RESID. These values are all the differences between the actual $y$-value of data points and the $y$-value calculated by the best-fit line or curve for that $x$-value. These values can be plotted on an $xy$-plane to produce a RESIDUAL PLOT. The residual plot helps determine if a line is the best model for the data. Residual points that are randomly dispersed above and below the horizontal indicate that a linear model is appropriate, while a $u$ shape or upside-down $u$ shape indicate a nonlinear model would be more appropriate.

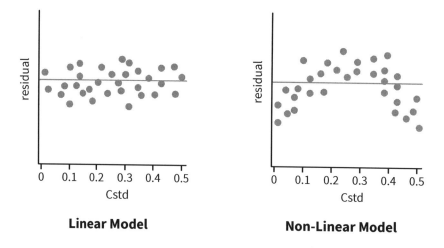

Figure 4.4. Residual Plots

Once a best-fit line is established, it can be used to estimate output values given an input value within the domain of the data. For a short extension outside that domain, reasonable predictions may be possible.

However, the further from the domain of the data the line is extended, the greater the reduction in the accuracy of the prediction.

It is important to note here that just because two variables have a strong positive or negative correlation, it cannot necessarily be inferred that those two quantities have a *causal* relationship—that is, that one variable changing *causes* the other quantity to change. There are often other factors that play into their relationship. For example, a positive correlation can be found between the number of ice cream sales and the number of shark attacks at a beach. It would be incorrect to say that selling more ice cream *causes* an increase in shark attacks. It is much more likely that on hot days more ice cream is sold, and many more people are swimming, so one of them is more likely to get attacked by a shark. Confusing correlation and causation is one of the most common statistical errors people make.

A graphing calculator can provide the regression line, *r* value, and residuals list.

## EXAMPLE

Based on the scatter plot below, where the *x*-axis represents hours spent studying per week and the *y*-axis represents the average percent grade on exams during the school year, is there a correlation between the amount of studying for a test and test results?

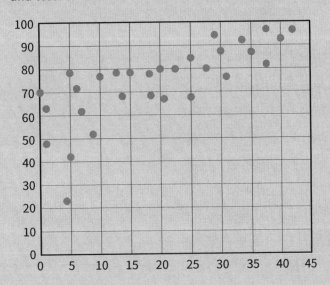

**Answer:**

**There is a somewhat weak positive correlation.** As the number of hours spent studying increases, the average percent grade also generally increases.

## Line Graphs

Line graphs are used to display a relationship between two variables, such as change over time. Like scatter plots, line graphs exist in quadrant I of the *xy*-plane. Line graphs are constructed by graphing each point and connecting each point to the next consecutive point by a line. To create a line graph, it may be necessary to consolidate data into single bivariate data points. Thus, a line graph is a function, with each *x*-value having exactly one *y*-value, whereas a scatter plot may have multiple *y*-values for one *x*-value.

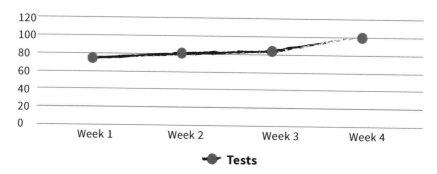

**Figure 4.5. Line Graph**

## EXAMPLE

Create a line graph based on the following survey values, where the first column represents an individual's age and the other represents that individual's reported happiness level on a 20-point scale (0 being the least happy that person has been and 20 being the happiest). Then interpret the resulting graph to determine whether the following statement is true or false: *On average, middle-aged people are less happy than young or older people are.*

| Age | Happiness |
|-----|-----------|
| 12 | 16 |
| 13 | 15 |
| 20 | 18 |
| 15 | 12 |
| 40 | 5 |
| 17 | 17 |
| 18 | 18 |
| 19 | 15 |
| 42 | 7 |
| 70 | 17 |
| 45 | 10 |
| 60 | 12 |
| 63 | 15 |
| 22 | 14 |
| 27 | 15 |

| Age | Happiness |
|---|---|
| 33 | 10 |
| 44 | 8 |
| 55 | 10 |
| 80 | 10 |
| 15 | 13 |
| 40 | 8 |
| 17 | 15 |
| 18 | 17 |
| 19 | 20 |
| 22 | 16 |
| 27 | 15 |
| 36 | 9 |
| 33 | 10 |
| 44 | 6 |

**Answer:**

To construct a line graph, the data must be ordered into consolidated categories by averaging the data of people who have the same age so that the data is one-to-one. For example, there are 2 twenty-two-year-olds who are reporting. Their average happiness level is 15. When all the data has been consolidated and ordered from least to greatest, the table and graph below can be presented.

| Age | Happiness |
|---|---|
| 12 | 16 |
| 13 | 15 |
| 15 | 12.5 |
| 17 | 16 |
| 18 | 17.5 |
| 19 | 17.5 |
| 20 | 18 |
| 22 | 15 |
| 27 | 15 |
| 33 | 10 |
| 36 | 10.5 |
| 40 | 6.5 |
| 42 | 7 |
| 44 | 7 |
| 45 | 10 |
| 55 | 10 |

| Age | Happiness |
|---|---|
| 60 | 12 |
| 63 | 15 |
| 70 | 17 |
| 80 | 10 |

**Average Happiness Rating Versus Age**

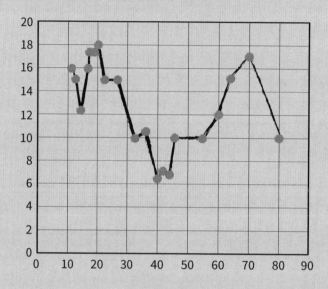

**The statement that, on average, middle-aged people are less happy than young or older people appears to be true.** According to the graph, people in their thirties, forties, and fifties are less happy than people in their teens, twenties, sixties, and seventies.

# Bar Graphs

Bar graphs compare differences between categories or changes over a time. The data is grouped into categories or ranges and represented by rectangles. A bar graph's rectangles can be vertical or horizontal, depending on whether the dependent variable is placed on the *x*- or *y*-axis. Instead of the *xy*-plane, however, one axis is made up of categories (or ranges) instead of a numeric scale. Bar graphs are useful

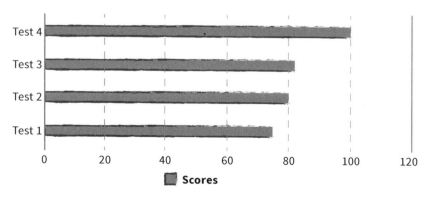

Figure 4.6. Bar Graph

because the differences between categories are easy to see: the height or length of each bar shows the value for each category.

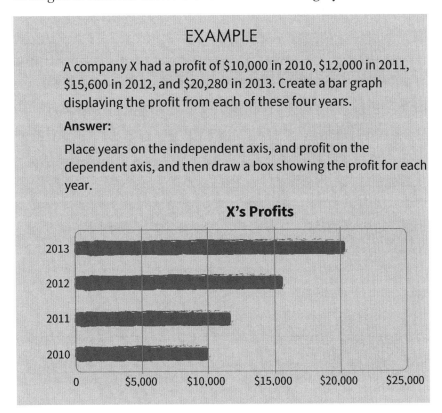

## EXAMPLE

A company X had a profit of $10,000 in 2010, $12,000 in 2011, $15,600 in 2012, and $20,280 in 2013. Create a bar graph displaying the profit from each of these four years.

**Answer:**

Place years on the independent axis, and profit on the dependent axis, and then draw a box showing the profit for each year.

## Stem-and-Leaf Plots

Stem-and-leaf plots are ways of organizing large amounts of data by grouping it into classes. All data points are broken into two parts: a stem and a leaf. For instance, the number 512 might be broken into a stem of 5 and a leaf of 12. All data in the 500 range would appear in the same row (this group of data is a class). Usually a simple key is provided to explain how the data is being represented. For instance, 5|12 = 512 would show that the stems are representing hundreds. The advantage of this display is that it shows general density and shape of the data in a compact display, yet all original data points are preserved and available. It is also easy to find medians and quartiles from this display.

| STEM | LEAF |
|------|------|
| 0 | 5 |
| 1 | 6, 7 |
| 2 | 8, 3, 6 |
| 3 | 4, 5, 9, 5, 5, 8, 5 |
| 4 | 7, 7, 7, 8 |
| 5 | 5, 4 |
| 6 | 0 |

Figure 4.7. Stem and Leaf Plot

The table gives the weights of wrestlers (in pounds) for a certain competition. What is the mean, median, and IQR of the data?

| 2 | 05, 22, 53, 40 |
|---|---|
| 3 | 07, 22, 29, 45, 89, 96, 98 |
| 4 | 10, 25, 34 |
| 6 | 21 |

Key: 2|05 = 205 pounds

**Answer:**

| | |
|---|---|
| $\mu = \dfrac{\Sigma x}{N}$ $= \dfrac{5281}{15}$ $= \textbf{353.1 lbs.}$ | Find the mean using the equation for the population mean. |
| Q1 = 253 Q2 = 345 Q3 = 410 IQR = 410 − 253 = 157 **The median is 345 lbs.** **The IQR is 157 lbs.** | Find the median and IQR by counting the leaves and identifying Q1, Q2, and Q3. |

## Frequency Tables and Histograms

The frequency of a particular data point is the number of times that data point occurs. Constructing a frequency table requires that the data or data classes be arranged in ascending order in one column and the frequency in another column.

A histogram is a graphical representation of a frequency table used to compare frequencies. A histogram is constructed in quadrant I of the *xy*-plane, with data in each equal-width class presented as a bar and the height of each bar representing the frequency of that class. Unlike bar graphs, histograms cannot have gaps between bars. A histogram is used to determine the distribution of data among the classes.

Histograms can be symmetrical, skewed left or right, or multimodal (data spread around). Note that SKEWED LEFT means the peak of the data is on the *right*, with a tail to the left, while SKEWED RIGHT means the peak is on the *left*, with a tail to the right. This seems counterintuitive to many; the "left" or "right" always refers to the tail of the data. This is because a long tail to the right, for example, means there are high outlier values that are skewing the data to the right.

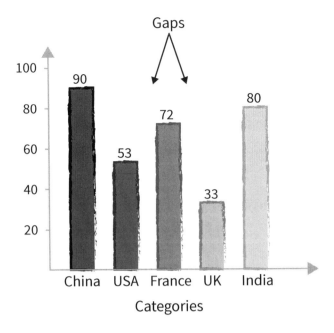

**Bar Chart**

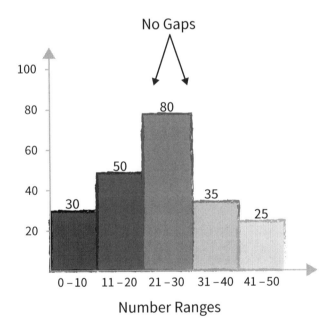

**Histogram**

**Figure 4.8. Bar Chart vs. Histogram**

A TWO-WAY FREQUENCY TABLE compares CATEGORICAL DATA (data in more than one category) of two related variables (bivariate data). Two-way frequency tables are also called CONTINGENCY TABLES and are often used to analyze survey results. One category is displayed along the top of the table and the other category down along the side. Rows and columns are added and the sums appear at the end of the row or column. The sum of all the row data must equal the sum of all the column data.

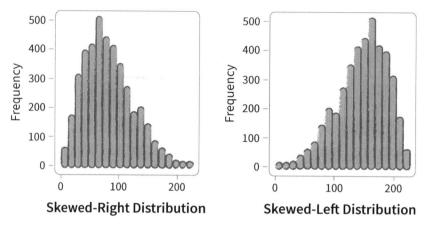

Figure 4.9. Histrograms

From a two-way frequency table, the JOINT RELATIVE FREQUENCY of a particular category can be calculated by taking the number in the row and column of the categories in question and dividing by the total number surveyed. This gives the percent of the total in that particular category. Sometimes the CONDITIONAL RELATIVE FREQUENCY is of interest. In this case, calculate the relative frequency confined to a single row or column.

Students by Grade and Gender

|  | 9TH GRADE | 10TH GRADE | 11TH GRADE | 12TH GRADE | TOTAL |
|---|---|---|---|---|---|
| Male | 57 | 63 | 75 | 61 | 256 |
| Female | 54 | 42 | 71 | 60 | 227 |
| Total | 111 | 105 | 146 | 121 | 483 |

Figure 4.10. Two-Way Frequency Table

## EXAMPLES

1) A café owner tracked the number of customers he had over a twelve-hour period in the following frequency table. Display the data in a histogram and determine what kind of distribution there is in the data.

| TIME | NUMBER OF CUSTOMERS |
|---|---|
| 6 a.m. – 8 a.m. | 5 |
| 8 a.m. – 9 a.m. | 6 |
| 9 a.m. – 10 a.m. | 5 |
| 10 a.m. – 12 p.m. | 23 |

| Time | Number of Customers |
|---|---|
| 12 p.m. – 2 p.m. | 24 |
| 2 p.m. – 4 p.m. | 9 |
| 4 p.m. – 6 p.m. | 4 |

**Answer:**

Since time is the independent variable, it is on the *x*-axis and the number of customers is on the *y*-axis. For the histogram to correctly display data continuously, categories on the *x*-axis must be equal 2-hour segments. The 8 a.m. – 9 a.m. and 9 a.m. – 10 a.m. categories must be combined for a total of 11 customers in that time period. Although not perfectly symmetrical, the amount of customers peaks in the middle and is therefore considered symmetrical.

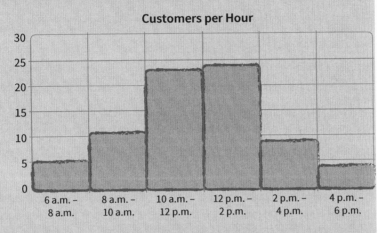

**Customers per Hour**

**2)** Cineflix movie theater polled its moviegoers on a weeknight to determine their favorite type of movie. The results are in the two-way frequency table below.

| Moviegoers | Comedy | Action | Horror | Totals |
|---|---|---|---|---|
| Male | 15 | 24 | 21 | 60 |
| Female | 8 | 18 | 17 | 43 |
| Totals | 23 | 42 | 38 | 103 |

Determine whether each of the following statements is true or false.

**A.** Action films are the most popular type of movie.

**B.** About 1 in 5 moviegoers prefers comedy films.

**C.** Men choose the horror genre more frequently than women do.

**Answer:**

A. **True**. More people (42) chose action movies than comedy (23) or horror (38).

**B.** **True**. Find the ratio of total number of people who prefer comedy to total number of people. $\frac{23}{103} = 0.22$; 1 in 5 is 20% so 22% is about the same.

**C.** **False**. The percentage of men who choose horror is less than the percentage of women who do.

*part = number of men who prefer horror* $= 21$

*whole = number of men surveyed* $= 60$

$percent = \frac{part}{whole}$

$= \frac{21}{60} = 0.35 = 35\%$

*part = number of women who prefer horror* $= 17$

*whole = number of women surveyed* $= 43$

$percent = \frac{part}{whole}$

$= \frac{17}{43} = 0.40 = 40\%$

five

# PROBABILITY

## Set Theory

A **SET** is any collection of items. In mathematics, a set is represented by a capital letter and described inside curly brackets. For example, if $S$ is the set of all integers less than 10, then $S = \{x|x$ is an integer and $x < 10\}$. The vertical bar $|$ is read *such that*. The set that contains no elements is called the **EMPTY SET** or the **NULL SET** and is denoted by empty brackets $\{\ \}$ or the symbol $\varnothing$.

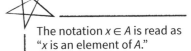

The notation $x \in A$ is read as "$x$ is an element of $A$."

Usually there is a larger set that any specific problem is based in, called the **UNIVERSAL SET** or **U**. For example, in the set $S$ described above, the universal set might be the set of all real numbers. The **COMPLEMENT** of set $A$, denoted by $\overline{A}$ or $A'$, is the set of all items in the universal set, but NOT in $A$. It can be helpful when working with sets to represent them with a **VENN DIAGRAM**.

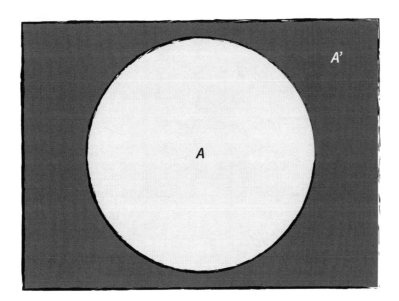

**Figure 5.1. Venn Diagram**

Oftentimes, the task will be working with multiple sets: *A*, *B*, *C*, etc. A **UNION** between two sets means that the data in both sets is combined into a single, larger set. The union of two sets, denoted $A \cup B$ contains all the data that is in either set *A* or set *B* or both (called an **INCLUSIVE OR**). If $A = \{1, 4, 7\}$ and $B = \{2, 4, 5, 8\}$, then $A \cup B = \{1, 2, 4, 5, 7, 8\}$ (notice 4 is included only once). The **INTERSECTION** of two sets, denoted $A \cap B$ includes only elements that are in both *A* and *B*. Thus, $A \cap B = \{4\}$ for the sets given above.

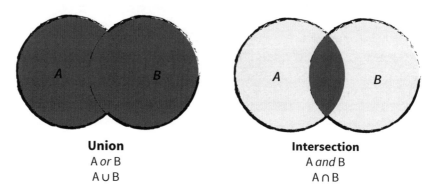

**Union**
A *or* B
A∪B

**Intersection**
A *and* B
A∩B

**Figure 5.2. Unions and Intersections**

If there is no common data in the sets in question, then the intersection is the null set. Two sets that have no elements in common (and thus have a null in the intersection set) are said to be **DISJOINT**. The **DIFFERENCE *B – A*** or **RELATIVE COMPLEMENT** between two sets is the set of all the values that are in *B*, but not in *A*. For the sets defined above, $B - A = \{2, 5, 8\}$ and $A - B = \{1, 7\}$. The relative complement is sometimes denoted as ***B\A***.

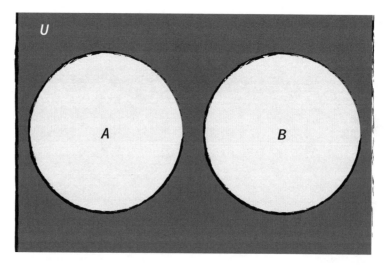

**Figure 5.3. Disjoint Sets**

Mathematical tasks often involve working with multiple sets. Just like numbers, sets and set operations have identities and properties.

## Set Identities

| | | |
|---|---|---|
| $A \cup \varnothing = A$ | $A \cup U = U$ | $A \cup \overline{A} = U$ |
| $A \cap \varnothing = A$ | $A \cap U = A$ | $A \cap \overline{A} = \varnothing$ |

## Set Properties

| | | |
|---|---|---|
| Commutative Property | $A \cup B = B \cup A$ | $A \cap B = B \cap A$ |
| Associative Property | $A \cup (B \cup C) =$ $(A \cup B) \cup C$ | $A \cap (B \cap C) = (A \cap B) \cap C$ |
| Distributive Property | $A \cup (B \cap C) =$ $(A \cup B) \cap (A \cup C)$ | $A \cap (B \cup C) =$ $(A \cap B) \cup (A \cap C)$ |

## De Morgan's Laws

$$\overline{(A \cup B)} = \overline{A} \cap \overline{B} \qquad \overline{(A \cap B)} = \overline{A} \cup \overline{B}$$

The number of elements in a set $A$ is denoted $n(A)$. For the set $A$ above, $n(A) = 3$, since there are three elements in that set. The number of elements in the union of two sets is $n(A \cup B) = n(A) + n(B) - n(A \cap B)$. Note that the number of elements in the intersection of the two sets must be subtracted because they are being counted twice, since they are both in set $A$ and in set $B$. The number of elements in the complement of $A$ is the number of elements in the universal set minus the number in set $A$: $n(\overline{A}) = n(U) - n(A)$.

It is helpful to note here how similar set theory is to the logic operators of the previous section: negation corresponds to complements, the "and" ($\wedge$) operator to intersection ($\cap$), and the "or" ($\vee$) operator to unions ($\cup$); notice even the symbols are similar.

## EXAMPLES

1) Construct a Venn diagram depicting the intersection, if any, of $Y = \{x \mid x$ is an integer and $0 < x < 9\}$ and $Z = \{-4, 0, 4, 8, 12, 16\}$.

**Answer:**

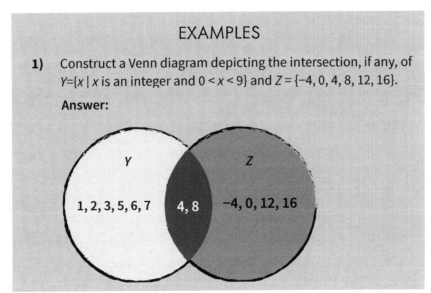

2) Suppose the universal set $U$ is the set of all integers between
   $-10$ and 10 inclusive. If $A = \{x \in U | x$ is a multiple of 5$\}$ and $B =$
   $\{x \in U | x$ is a multiple of 2$\}$ are subsets within the universal set,
   find $\overline{A}$, $A \cup B$ and $A \cap B$, and $\overline{A} \cap \overline{B}$.

   **A.** $\overline{A}$

   **B.** $A \cup B$

   **C.** $A \cap B$

   **D.** $\overline{A} \cap \overline{B}$

   **Answer:**

   A. $\overline{A}$ includes all elements of the universal set that are not in
      set $A$:
      $\overline{A} = \{-9, -8, -7, -6, -4, -3, -2, -1, 1, 2, 3, 4, 6, 7, 8, 9\}$.

   B. $A \cup B$ is all elements in either $A$ or $B$:
      $A \cup B = \{-10, -5, 0, 5, 10, -8, -6, -4, -2, 2, 4, 6, 8\}$

   C. $A \cap B$ is all elements in both $A$ and $B$:
      $A \cap B = \{-10, 0, 10\}$

   D. $\overline{A} \cap \overline{B}$ is all the elements of the universal set that are not in
      either $A$ or $B$:
      $\overline{A} \cap \overline{B} = \{-9, -7, -3, -1, 1, 3, 7, 9\}$

# Probability

Probability describes how likely something is to happen. In probability, an **EVENT** is the single result of a trial, and an **OUTCOME** is a possible event that results from a trial. The collection of all possible outcomes for a particular trial is called the **SAMPLE SPACE**. For example, when rolling a die, the sample space is the numbers $1 - 6$. Rolling a single number, such as 4, would be a single event.

## Counting Principles

Counting principles are methods used to find the number of possible outcomes for a given situation. The **FUNDAMENTAL COUNTING PRINCIPLE** states that, for a series of independent events, the number of outcomes can be found by multiplying the number of possible outcomes for each event. For example, if a die is rolled (6 possible outcomes) and a coin is tossed (2 possible outcomes), there are $6 \times 2 = 12$ total possible outcomes.

Combinations and permutations describe how many ways a number of objects taken from a group can be arranged. The number of objects in the group is written $n$, and the number of objects to be arranged is represented by $r$ (or $k$). In a **combination**, the order of the selections does not matter because every available slot to be filled is the same. Examples of combinations include:

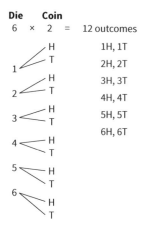

**Figure 5.4. Fundamental
Counting Principle**

- picking 3 people from a group of 12 to form a committee (220 possible committees)
- picking 3 pizza toppings from 10 options (120 possible pizzas)

In a **PERMUTATION**, the order of the selection matters, meaning each available slot is different. Examples of permutations include:

- handing out gold, silver, and bronze medals in a race with 100 participants (970,200 possible combinations)
- selecting a president, vice-president, secretary, and treasurer from among a committee of 12 people (11,880 possible combinations)

The formulas for the both calculations are similar. The only difference—the $r!$ in the denominator of a combination—accounts for redundant outcomes. Note that both permutations and combinations can be written in several different shortened notations.

$$\text{Permutation: } P(n, r) = {}_nP_r = \frac{n!}{(n-r)!}$$

$$\text{Combination: } C(n, r) = {}_nC_r = \binom{n}{r} = \frac{n!}{(n-r)!r!}$$

## EXAMPLES

**1)** A personal assistant is struggling to pick a shirt, tie, and cufflink set that go together. If his client has 70 shirts, 2 ties, and 5 cufflinks, how many possible combinations does he have to consider?

**Answer:**

Multiply the number of outcomes for each individual event:

$(70)(2)(5) = $ **700 outfits**

**2)** If there are 20 applicants for 3 open positions, in how many different ways can a team of 3 be hired?

**Answer:**

The order of the items doesn't matter, so use the formula for combinations:

$$C(n, r) = \frac{n!}{(n-r)!r!}$$

$$C(20, 3) = \frac{20!}{(20-3)!3!}$$

$$= \frac{20!}{(17!\ 3!)}$$

$$= \frac{(20)(19)(18)}{3!} = \textbf{1140 possible teams}$$

**3)** Calculate the number of unique permutations that can be made with five of the letters in the word *pickle*.

**Answer:**

To find the number of unique permutations of 5 letters in pickle, use the permutation formula:

$$P(n,r) = \frac{n!}{(n-r)!}$$

$$P(6,5) = \frac{6!}{(6-5)!}$$

$$= \frac{720}{1} = \mathbf{720}$$

**4)** Find the number of permutations that can be made out of all the letters in the word *cheese*.

**Answer:**

The letter *e* repeats 3 times in the word *cheese*, meaning some permutations of the 6 letters will be indistinguishable from others. The number of permutations must be divided by the number of ways the three *e*'s can be arranged to account for these redundant outcomes:

$$total\ number\ of\ permutations = \frac{number\ of\ ways\ of\ arranging\ 6\ letters}{number\ of\ ways\ of\ arranging\ 3\ letters}$$

$$= \frac{6!}{3!} = 6 \times 5 \times 4 = \mathbf{120}$$

# Probability of a Single Event

The probability of a single event occurring is the number of outcomes in which that event occurs (called **FAVORABLE EVENTS**) divided by the number of items in the sample space (total possible outcomes):

$$P\ (an\ event) = \frac{number\ of\ favorable\ outcomes}{total\ number\ of\ possible\ outcomes}$$

The probability of any event occurring will always be a fraction or decimal between 0 and 1. It may also be expressed as a percent. An event with 0 probability will never occur and an event with a probability of 1 is certain to occur. The probability of an event not occurring is referred to as that event's **COMPLEMENT**. The sum of an event's probability and the probability of that event's complement will always be 1.

## EXAMPLES

**1)** What is the probability that an even number results when a six-sided die is rolled? What is the probability the die lands on 5?

**Answer:**

$$P(rolling\ even) = \frac{number\ of\ favorable\ outcomes}{total\ number\ of\ possible\ outcomes} = \frac{3}{6} = \frac{1}{2}$$

$$P(rolling\ 5) = \frac{number\ of\ favorable\ outcomes}{total\ number\ of\ possible\ outcomes} = \mathbf{\frac{1}{6}}$$

**2)** Only 20 tickets were issued in a raffle. If someone were to buy 6 tickets, what is the probability that person would not win the raffle?

**Answer:**

$$P(not\ winning) = \frac{number\ of\ favorable\ outcomes}{total\ number\ of\ possible\ outcomes} = \frac{14}{20} = \frac{7}{10}$$

or

$$P(not\ winning) = 1 - P(winning) = 1 - \frac{6}{20} = \frac{14}{20} = \mathbf{\frac{7}{10}}$$

**3)** A bag contains 26 tiles representing the 26 letters of the English alphabet. If 3 tiles are drawn from the bag without replacement, what is the probability that all 3 will be consonants?

**Answer:**

$$P = \frac{\text{number of favorable outcomes}}{\text{total number of possible outcomes}}$$

$$= \frac{\text{number of 3-consonant combinations}}{\text{number of 3-tile combinations}}$$

$$= \frac{_{21}C_3}{_{26}C_3}$$

$$= \frac{1330}{2600}$$

$$= 0.511 = \mathbf{51\%}$$

# Probability of Multiple Events

If events are INDEPENDENT, the probability of one occurring does not affect the probability of the other event occurring. Rolling a die and getting one number does not change the probability of getting any particular number on the next roll. The number of faces has not changed, so these are independent events.

If events are DEPENDENT, the probability of one occurring changes the probability of the other event occurring. Drawing a card from a deck without replacing it will affect the probability of the next card drawn because the number of available cards has changed.

To find the probability that two or more independent events will occur (*A* and *B*), simply multiply the probabilities of each individual event together. To find the probability that one, the other, or both will occur (*A* or *B*), it's necessary to add their probabilities and then subtract their overlap (which prevents the same values from being counted twice).

CONDITIONAL PROBABILITY is the probability of an event occurring given that another event has occurred. The notation $P(B|A)$ represents the probability that event *B* occurs, given that event *A* has already occurred (it is read "probability of *B*, given *A*").

When drawing objects, the phrase *with replacement* describes independent events, and *without replacement* describes dependent events.

Table 5.1. Probability Formulas

| INDEPENDENT EVENTS | | DEPENDENT EVENTS |
|---|---|---|
| Intersection *and* | Union *or* | Conditional |
| $P(A \cap B) = P(A) \times P(B)$ | $P(A \cup B) = P(A) + P(B) - P(A \cap B)$ | $P(B|A) = P(A \cap B)/P(A)$ |

Two events that are MUTUALLY EXCLUSIVE CANNOT happen at the same time. This is similar to disjoint sets in set theory. The probability that two mutually exclusive events will occur is zero. MUTUALLY INCLUSIVE events share common outcomes.

## EXAMPLES

1) A card is drawn from a standard 52 card deck. What is the probability that it is either a queen or a heart?

**Answer:**

This is a union (*or*) problem.

$P(A)$ = the probability of drawing a queen = $\frac{1}{13}$

$P(B)$ = the probability of drawing a heart = $\frac{1}{4}$

$P(A \cap B)$ = the probability of drawing a heart and a queen = $\frac{1}{52}$

$P(A \cup B) = P(A) + P(B) - P(A \cap B)$

$= \frac{1}{13} + \frac{1}{4} - \frac{1}{52}$

$= \mathbf{0.31}$

2) A group of ten individuals is drawing straws from a group of 28 long straws and 2 short straws. If the straws are not replaced, what is the probability, as a percentage, that neither of the first two individuals will draw a short straw?

**Answer:**

This scenario includes two events, $A$ and $B$.

The probability of the first person drawing a long straw is an independent event:

$P(A) = \frac{28}{30}$

The probability the second person draws a long straw changes because one long straw has already been drawn. In other words, it is the probability of event $B$ given that event $A$ has already happened:

$P(B|A) = \frac{27}{29}$

The conditional probability formula can be used to determine the probability of both people drawing long straws:

$P(A \cap B) = P(A)P(B|A)$

$= \left(\frac{28}{30}\right)\left(\frac{27}{29}\right)$

$= 0.87$

There is an **87% chance** that neither of the first two individuals will draw short straws.

# Binomial Probability

A binomial (or Bernoulli) trial is an experiment with exactly two mutually exclusive outcomes (often labeled success and failure) where the probability of each outcome is constant. The probability of success is given as $p$, and the probability of failure is $q = 1 - p$. The BINOMIAL PROBABILITY formula can be used to determine the probability of getting a certain number of successes ($r$) within a given number of trials ($n$). These values can also be used to find the expected value ($\mu$), or mean, of the trial, and its standard deviation ($\sigma$).

$$P = {}_nC_r(p^r)(q^{n-r})$$

$$\mu = np$$

$$\sigma = \sqrt{np(1-p)}$$

## EXAMPLE

What is the probability of rolling a five on a standard 6-sided die 4 times in 10 tries?

**Answer:**

| | |
|---|---|
| $p = \frac{1}{6}$ $q = \frac{5}{6}$ $n = 10$ $r = 4$ | Identify the variables given in the problem. |
| $P = {}_nC_r(p^r)(q^{n-r})$ $= \left(\frac{10!}{(10-4)!4!}\right)\left(\frac{1}{6}\right)^4\left(\frac{5}{6}\right)^{10-4}$ $= 0.054$ There is a **5.4% chance**. | Plug these values into the binomial probability formula. |

# PART II: PRACTICE

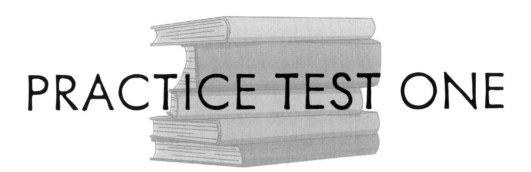

# PRACTICE TEST ONE

Directions: Read the problem carefully, and choose the best answer.

1) If $j = 4$, what is the value of
$2(j-4)^4 - j + \frac{1}{2}j$ ?

  A. 0

  B. −2

  C. 2

  D. 4

  E. 32

2) Line $a$ and line $b$ are perpendicular and intersect at the point $(-100, 100)$. If $(-95, 115)$ is a point on line $b$, which of the following could be a point on line $a$?

  A. $(-112, -104)$

  B. $(-112, 104)$

  C. $(-100, -95)$

  D. $(-95, 115)$

  E. $(104, 168)$

3) Simplify: $(5 + 2i)(3 + 4i)$

  A. 7

  B. 23

  C. $7 + 26i$

  D. $23 + 26i$

  E. $7 - 26i$

4) Which inequality is represented by the following graph?

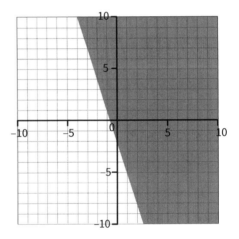

  A. $y \geq -3x - 2$

  B. $y \geq 3x - 2$

  C. $y > -3x - 2$

  D. $y \leq -3x - 2$

  E. $y \geq -3x + 2$

5) Simplify: $\frac{7.2 \times 10^6}{1.6 \times 10^{-3}}$

  A. $4.5 \times 10^{-9}$

  B. $4.5 \times 10^{-3}$

  C. $4.5 \times 10^{-2}$

  D. $4.5 \times 10^3$

  E. $4.5 \times 10^9$

**6)** If △*ABD* ~ △*DEF* and the similarity ratio is 3:4, what is the measure of *DE* if *AB* = 12?

    **A.** 6

    **B.** 9

    **C.** 12

    **D.** 16

    **E.** 96

**7)** Which of the following could be the perimeter of a triangle with two sides that measure 13 and 5?

    **A.** 24.5

    **B.** 26.5

    **C.** 36

    **D.** 37

    **E.** 37.5

**8)** What is the relationship between the mean and the median in a data set that is skewed right?

    **A.** The mean is greater than the median.

    **B.** The mean is less than the median.

    **C.** The mean and median are equal.

    **D.** The mean may be greater than or equal to the median.

    **E.** The mean may be less than or equal to the median.

**9)** The average speed of cars on a highway (*s*) is inversely proportional to the number of cars on the road (*n*). If a car drives at 65 mph when there are 250 cars on the road, how fast will a car drive when there are 325 cars on the road?

    **A.** 50 mph

    **B.** 55 mph

    **C.** 60 mph

    **D.** 85 mph

    **E.** 87 mph

**10)** Simplify: $-(3^2) + (5 - 7)^2 - 3(4 - 8)$

    **A.** −25

    **B.** −17

    **C.** −1

    **D.** 7

    **E.** 25

**11)** In the figure below, there are six line segments that terminate at point *O*. If segment $\overline{DO}$ bisects ∠*AOF* and segment $\overline{BO}$ bisects ∠*AOD*, what is the value of ∠*AOF*?

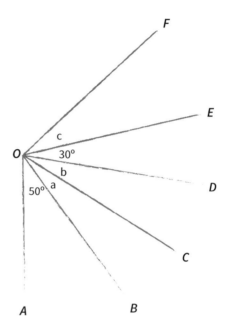

    **A.** 140°

    **B.** 150°

    **C.** 160°

    **D.** 170°

    **E.** 200°

**12)** A pair of 6-sided dice is rolled 10 times. What is the probability that in exactly 3 of those rolls, the sum of the dice will be 5?

    **A.** 0.14%

    **B.** 7.2%

    **C.** 11.1%

    **D.** 30%

    **E.** 60%

**13)** 600 people between the ages of 15 and 45 were polled regarding their use of social media. 200 people from each age group were part of the study. The results are listed in the relative frequency table below.

Hours Per Day Spent on Social Media

| AGE (YEARS) | LESS THAN 2 HOURS | 2 TO 4 HOURS | MORE THAN 4 HOURS | TOTAL |
|---|---|---|---|---|
| 15 – 25 | 0.15 | 0.40 | 0.45 | 1.0 |
| 25 – 35 | 0.52 | 0.28 | 0.20 | 1.0 |
| 35 – 45 | 0.85 | 0.10 | 0.05 | 1.0 |
| **Total** | 0.51 | 0.26 | 0.23 | 1.0 |

Which of the statements are true?

I.   Of people 25 to 35 years old, 20% spend more than 4 hours per day on social media.

II.  Of the population of 15 to 45-year-olds, 26% spend 2 – 4 hours a day on social media.

III. Of people between the ages of 15 and 35, 67% spend 0 – 2 hours per day on social media.

IV.  5 people who reported using social media more than 4 hours per week were 35 to 45 years old.

A. II only

B. I and II

C. I, II, and IV

D. I, II, and III

E. II, III, and IV

**14)** Which of the following is equivalent to $z^3(z+2)^2 - 4z^3 + 2$?

A. $2$

B. $z^5 + 4z^4 + 4z^3 + 2$

C. $z^6 + 4z^3 + 2$

D. $z^5 + 4z^4 + 2$

E. $z^5 + 4z^3 + 6$

**15)** A high school cross country team sent 25 percent of its runners to a regional competition. Of these, 10 percent won medals. If 2 runners earned medals, how many members does the cross country team have?

A. 8

B. 10

C. 80

D. 125

E. 1250

**16)** Which value is equivalent to $5^2 \times (-5)^{-2} - (2+3)^{-1}$?

A. $0$

B. $\frac{4}{5}$

C. $1$

D. $\frac{5}{4}$

E. $2$

**17)** If the length of a rectangle is increased by 40% and its width is decreased by 40%, what is the effect on the rectangle's area?

A. The area is the same.

B. It increases by 16%.

C. It increases by 20%.

D. It decreases by 16%.

E. It decreases by 20%.

**18)** The pie graph below shows how a state's government plans to spend its annual budget of $3 billion. How much more money does the state plan to spend on infrastructure than education?

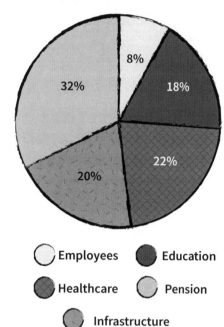

- **Employees**
- **Education**
- **Healthcare**
- **Pension**
- **Infrastructure**

A. $60,000,000
B. $120,000,000
C. $300,000,000
D. $540,000,000
E. $600,000,000

**19)** Simplify: 6! + 0! + 1!

A. 720
B. 721
C. 722
D. 723
E. 724

**20)** Find the 12th term of the following sequence.

−57, −40, −23, −6...

A. 57
B. 79
C. 113
D. 130
E. 147

**21)** In a theater, there are 4,500 lower-level seats and 2,000 upper-level seats. What is the ratio of lower-level seats to total seats?

A. $\frac{4}{9}$

B. $\frac{4}{13}$

C. $\frac{9}{13}$

D. $\frac{9}{4}$

E. $\frac{13}{9}$

**22)** Fifteen DVDs are to be arranged on a shelf. 4 of the DVDs are horror films, 6 are comedies, and 5 are science fiction. In how many ways can the DVDs be arranged if DVDs of the same genre must be placed together?

A. 1,800
B. 2,073,600
C. 6,220,800
D. 12,441,600
E. 131,216,200

**23)** $W$, $X$, $Y$, and $Z$ lie on a circle with center $A$. If the diameter of the circle is 75, what is the sum of $\overline{AW}$, $\overline{AX}$, $\overline{AY}$, and $\overline{AZ}$?

A. 75
B. 100
C. 125
D. 300
E. 150

**24)** If a person reads 40 pages in 45 minutes, approximately how many minutes will it take her to read 265 pages?

A. 202
B. 236
C. 265
D. 298
E. 300

25) If an employee who makes $37,500 per year receives a 5.5% raise, what is the employee's new salary?

A. $35,437.50

B. $35,625.00

C. $39,375.00

D. $39,562.50

E. $58,125.00

26) Points $B$ and $C$ are on a circle. Point $A$ is located such that the line segments $\overline{AB}$ and $\overline{AC}$ are congruent. Which of the following could be true?

I. $A$ is the center of the circle.

II. $A$ is on arc $\overparen{BC}$.

III. $A$ is outside of the circle.

A. I

B. I and II

C. I and III

D. II and III

E. I, II, and III

27) If angles $a$ and $b$ are congruent, what is the measurement of angle $c$?

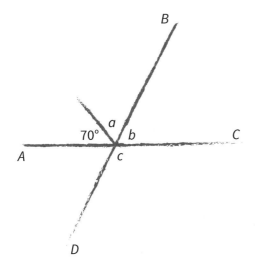

A. 55°

B. 70°

C. 110°

D. 120°

E. 125°

28) Which of the following is a solution of the given equation?

$$4(m + 4)^2 - 4m^2 + 20 = 276$$

A. 3

B. 4

C. 6

D. 12

E. 24

29) Which of the following is the $y$-intercept of the given equation?

$$7y - 42x + 7 = 0$$

A. $(0, \frac{1}{6})$

B. $(6, 0)$

C. $(0, -1)$

D. $(-1, 0)$

E. $(0, 7)$

30) $\overline{MN}$ is the diameter of circle $O$. If the coordinates of $M$ are $(4, 5)$ and the coordiantes of $N$ are $(-12, -11)$, what is the equation for circle $O$?

A. $(x + 4)^2 + (y + 3)^2 = 100$

B. $(x - 3)^2 + (y - 4)^2 = 10$

C. $(x + 4)^2 + (y - 3)^2 = 10$

D. $(x - 4)^2 + (y + 3)^2 = 100$

E. $(x + 3)^2 + (y + 4)^2 = 100$

31) Which statement about the following set is true?

$$\{60, 5, 18, 20, 37, 37, 11, 90, 72\}$$

A. The median and the mean are equal.

B. The mean is less than the mode.

C. The mode is greater than the median.

D. The median is less than the mean.

E. The mode and the mean are equal.

**32)** If the volume of a cube is 343 cubic meters, what is the cube's surface area?

**A.** 49 m²

**B.** 84 m²

**C.** 196 m²

**D.** 294 m²

**E.** 343 m²

**33)** In the *xy*-coordinate plane, how many points have a distance of four from the origin?

**A.** 0

**B.** 1

**C.** 2

**D.** 4

**E.** ∞

**34)** 50 shares of a financial stock and 10 shares of an auto stock are valued at $1,300. If 10 shares of the financial stock and 10 shares of the auto stock are valued at $500, what is the value of 50 shares of the auto stock?

**A.** $30

**B.** $20

**C.** $1,300

**D.** $1,500

**E.** $1,800

**35)** Which of the following is listed in order from greatest to least?

**A.** $\frac{1}{2}, \frac{1}{3}, \frac{1}{7}, -\frac{1}{5}, -\frac{1}{6}, -\frac{1}{4}$

**B.** $\frac{1}{2}, \frac{1}{3}, \frac{1}{7}, -\frac{1}{6}, -\frac{1}{5}, -\frac{1}{4}$

**C.** $\frac{1}{2}, \frac{1}{7}, \frac{1}{3}, -\frac{1}{4}, -\frac{1}{5}, -\frac{1}{6}$

**D.** $\frac{1}{2}, \frac{1}{3}, \frac{1}{7}, -\frac{1}{6}, -\frac{1}{4}, -\frac{1}{5}$

**E.** $\frac{1}{2}, \frac{1}{3}, \frac{1}{7}, -\frac{1}{4}, -\frac{1}{5}, -\frac{1}{6}$

**36)** Simplify: $\frac{(3x^2y^2)^2}{3^3x^{-2}y^3}$

**A.** $3x^6y$

**B.** $\frac{x^6y}{3}$

**C.** $\frac{x^4}{3y}$

**D.** $\frac{3x^4}{y}$

**E.** $\frac{x^6y}{3}$

**37)** If △*ABC* is rotated counterclockwise 180° about point *A*, what are the coordinates of the new triangle?

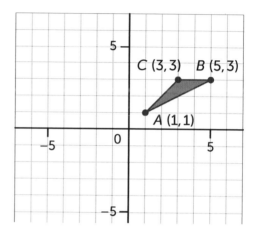

**A.** $A'(1, 1), B'(-3, -1), C'(-1, -1)$

**B.** $A'(-1, -1), B'(-5, -1), C'(-3, -3)$

**C.** $A'(1, 1), B'(-5, -1), C'(-3, -3)$

**D.** $A'(-1, -1), B'(-3, -1), C'(-1, -1)$

**E.** $A'(1, 1), B'(1, 5), C'(3, 3)$

**38)** The population of a city in 2008 was 1.25 million people. If the population is decreasing by 5% annually, in what year will the population reach 1 million?

**A.** 2011

**B.** 2012

**C.** 2013

**D.** 2014

**E.** 2015

**39)** Rectangular water tank A is 5 feet long, 10 feet wide, and 4 feet tall. Rectangular tank B is 5 feet long, 5 feet wide, and 4 feet tall. If the same amount of water is poured into both tanks and the height of the water in Tank A is 1 foot, how high will the water be in Tank B?

A. 1 foot

B. 2 feet

C. 3 feet

D. 4 feet

E. 5 feet

**40)** Simplify: $\sqrt[3]{64} + \sqrt[3]{729}$

A. 13

B. 15

C. 17

D. 31

E. 35

**41)** In a class of 20 students, how many conversations must be had so that every student talks to every other student in the class?

A. 40

B. 190

C. 380

D. 760

E. 6840

**42)** Which of the following is the solution set to the given inequality?

$2x + 4 \geq 5(x - 4) - 3(x - 4)$

A. $(-\infty, \infty)$

B. $(-\infty, 6.5]$

C. $[6.5, -\infty)$

D. $(-\infty, 6.5) \cup (6.5, \infty)$

E. $\varnothing$

**43)** If $B = \begin{bmatrix} 6 & 4 \\ 8 & -2 \\ 5 & -3 \end{bmatrix}$ and $C = \begin{bmatrix} -2 & 5 \\ 7 & 1 \\ -4 & 4 \end{bmatrix}$, find $B + C$.

A. $\begin{bmatrix} 4 & 9 \\ 15 & -1 \\ -1 & -1 \end{bmatrix}$

B. $\begin{bmatrix} 4 & 9 \\ 15 & -1 \\ 1 & 1 \end{bmatrix}$

C. $\begin{bmatrix} 4 & 9 \\ 15 & 1 \\ 1 & 1 \end{bmatrix}$

D. $\begin{bmatrix} -4 & -9 \\ -15 & 1 \\ -1 & -1 \end{bmatrix}$

E. These matrices cannot be added.

**44)** What is the solution set for the inequality $2x^2 - 4x - 6 < 0$?

A. $(-1, 3)$

B. $(-\infty, \infty)$

C. $\varnothing$

D. $(-\infty, -1) \cup (3, \infty)$

E. $(-1, \infty)$

**45)** If the perimeter of an equilateral triangle is 30 inches, what is the altitude of the triangle?

A. 5

B. $5\sqrt{3}$

C. 10

D. $15\sqrt{3}$

E. $30\sqrt{3}$

**46)** What are the roots of the equation $y = 16x^3 - 48x^2$?

A. $\left\{ \frac{3+i\sqrt{5}}{2}, \frac{3-i\sqrt{5}}{2} \right\}$

B. $\{0, 3, -3\}$

C. $\{0, 3i, -3i\}$

D. $\{0, 3\}$

E. $\{0\}$

**47)** If $D = \begin{bmatrix} 3 & 7 \\ 4 & 9 \end{bmatrix}$, find det(**D**).

A. −2

B. −1

C. 0

D. 1

E. 2

**48)** Which of the following are the vertical asymptotes of the given function?

$$f(x) = \frac{x^3 - 16x}{-4x^2 + 4x + 24}$$

A. $x = -4$ and $x = 4$

B. $x = -3$ and $x = 2$

C. $x = -2$ and $x = 3$

D. $x = 0$ and $x = 4$

E. $x = 0$ and $x = 2$

**49)** If $\triangle JKL \sim \triangle PQR$ and $JK = 10$, $KL = 18.2$, $JL = 13.4$, and $QR = 47.1$, what is the approximate perimeter of $\triangle PQR$?

A. 42

B. 80

C. 89

D. 108

E. 135

**50)** The mean of 13 numbers is 30. The mean of 8 of these numbers is 42. What is the mean of the other 5 numbers?

A. 5.5

B. 10.8

C. 16.4

D. 21.2

E. 30.0

# ANSWER KEY

**1)**

**B.** Plug 4 in for $j$ and simplify.

$2(j-4)^4 - j + \frac{1}{2}j$

$2(4-4)^4 - 4 + \frac{1}{2}(4) = \mathbf{-2}$

**2)**

**C.** Find the slope of line $b$, take the negative reciprocal to find the slope of $a$, and test each point.

$(x_1, y_1) = (-100, 100)$

$(x_2, y_2) = (-95, 115)$

$m_b = \frac{115-100}{-95-(-100)} = \frac{15}{5} = 3$

$m_a = -\frac{1}{3}$

$(-112, -104)$: $\frac{100-(-104)}{-100-(-112)} = 17$

$(-112, 104)$: $\frac{100-104}{-100-(-112)} = \mathbf{-\frac{1}{3}}$

$(-100, -95)$: $\frac{100-(-100)}{-100-(-95)} = 40$

$(-95, 115)$: $\frac{100-115}{-100-(-95)} = 3$

$(104, 168)$: $\frac{100-168}{-100-(104)} = \frac{1}{3}$

**3)**

**C.** FOIL and combine like terms.

$(5+2i)(3+4i)$

$= 15 + 6i + 20i + 8i^2$

$= 15 + 6i + 20i + (8)(-1)$

$= 15 + 6i + 20i - 8$

$= \mathbf{7 + 26i}$

**4)**

Eliminate answer choices that don't match the graph.

**A.** Correct.

B. The graph has a negative slope while this inequality has a positive slope.

C. The line on the graph is solid, so the inequality should include the "or equal to" symbol.

D. The shading is above the line, meaning the inequality should be "$y$ is greater than."

E. The $y$-intercept is $-2$, not 2.

**5)**

**E.** Divide the digits and subtract the exponents.

$\frac{7.2 \times 10^6}{1.6 \times 10^{-3}}$

$7.2 \div 1.6 = 4.5$

$6 - (-3) = 9$

$\mathbf{4.5 \times 10^9}$

**6)**

**D.** Set up a proportion and solve.

$\frac{AB}{DE} = \frac{3}{4}$

$\frac{12}{DE} = \frac{3}{4}$

$3(DE) = 48$

$\mathbf{DE = 16}$

**7)**

**B.** Use the triangle inequality theorem to find the possible values for the third side, then calculate the possible perimeters.

$13 - 5 < s < 13 + 5$

$8 < s < 18$

$13 + 5 + 8 < P < 13 + 5 + 18$

$26 < P < 36$

**26.5 is the only answer choice in this range.**

### 8)

**A.** If the data is skewed right, the set includes extremes values that are to the right, or high. The median is unaffected by these high values, but the mean includes these high values and would therefore be greater.

### 9)

**A.** Use the formula for inversely proportional relationships to find $k$ and then solve for $s$.

$sn = k$

$(65)(250) = k$

$k = 16{,}250$

$s(325) = 16{,}250$

$s = \mathbf{50}$

### 10)

**D.** Simplify using PEMDAS.

$-(3^2) + (5 - 7)^2 - 3(4 - 8)$

$= -(3^2) + (-2)^2 - 3(-4)$

$= -9 + 4 - 3(-4)$

$= -9 + 4 + 12 = \mathbf{7}$

### 11)

**E.** Set up a system of equations.

$OD$ bisects $\angle AOF$: $50 + a + b = 30 + c$

$BO$ bisects $\angle AOD$: $50 = a + b$

Substitute and solve.

$50 + 50 = 30 + c$

$c = 70$

Add each angle to find m$\angle AOF$.

$\angle AOF = 50° + a° + b° + 30° + c°$

$\angle AOF = 50° + 50° + 30° + 70°$

$\angle AOF = \mathbf{200°}$

### 12)

**B.** Use the equation for Bernoulli trials (binomial distribution).

$P = {}_nC_r(p^r)(q^{n-r})$

$n = 10$

$r = 3$

$p = \dfrac{4}{36} = \dfrac{1}{9}$

$q = \dfrac{8}{9}$

$P = {}_{10}C_3\left(\dfrac{1}{9}\right)^3\left(\dfrac{8}{9}\right)^7 = 0.072 = \mathbf{7.2\%}$

### 13)

**B.** I. True: The row "25 – 35 year-olds" and the column "more than 4 hours" show a relative frequency of 0.20 or 20%.

II. True: The total relative frequency of participants who spend 2 to 4 hours on social media a day is 0.26 or 26%.

III. False: These percentages cannot be added because the "whole" is not the same. To calculate the percentage of people aged 15 – 35 who use social media less than 2 hours a day, find the total number of people in each category and divide by the total number of people in both categories.

*people 15 – 25 years old spending < 2 hrs.* = $0.15(200) = 30$

*people 25 – 35 years old spending < 2 hrs.* = $0.52(200) = 104$

*percentage of people 15 – 35 years old spending < 2 hrs.* = $\dfrac{30 + 104}{400} = 0.34 = 34\%$

IV. False: The number of people aged 35 – 45 who used social media more than 4 hours a day is $0.05(200) = 10$.

### 14)

**D.** Simplify using PEMDAS.

$z^3(z + 2)^2 - 4z^3 + 2$

$z^3(z^2 + 4z + 4) - 4z^3 + 2$

$z^5 + 4z^4 + 4z^3 - 4z^3 + 2$

$\mathbf{z^5 + 4z^4 + 2}$

### 15)

**C.** Work backwards to find the number of runners in the competition ($c$) and then the number of runners on the team ($r$).

$\dfrac{2}{c} = \dfrac{10}{100}$

$c = 20$

$\dfrac{20}{r} = \dfrac{25}{100}$

$\mathbf{r = 80}$

### 16)

**B.** Simplify using PEMDAS.

$5^2 \times (-5)^{-2} - 5^{-1}$

$= 25 \times \dfrac{1}{25} - \dfrac{1}{5}$

$= 1 - \frac{1}{5}$

$= \frac{4}{5}$

**17)**

**D.** Use the formula for the area of a rectangle to find the increase in its size.

$A = lw$

$A = (1.4l)(0.6w)$

$A = 0.84lw$

The new area will be 84% of the original area, a decrease of **16%**.

**18)**

**A.** Find the amount the state will spend on infrastructure and education, and then find the difference.

*infrastructure* = 0.2(3,000,000,000) = 600,000,000

*education* = 0.18(3,000,000,000) = 540,000,000

600,000,000 − 540,000,000 = **$60,000,000**

**19)**

**C.** Calculate each factorial and multiply.

$6! = 6 \times 5 \times 4 \times 3 \times 2 \times 1 = 720$

$0! = 1$

$1! = 1$

720 + 1 + 1 = **722**

**20)**

**D.** Use the equation to find the *n*th term of an arithmetic sequence.

$a_1 = -57$

$d = -40 - (-57) = 17$

$n = 12$

$a_n = a_1 + d(n - 1)$

$a_{12} = -57 + 17(12 - 1)$

$\boldsymbol{a_{12} = 130}$

**21)**

**C.**

total seats = 4,500 + 2,000

$\frac{\text{lower seats}}{\text{all seats}} = \frac{4,500}{6,500} = \frac{9}{13}$

**22)**

**D.** Use the fundamental counting principle to determine how many ways the DVDs can be

arranged within each category and how many ways the 3 categories can be arranged.

*ways to arrange horror* = 4! = 24

*ways to arrange comedies* = 6! = 720

*ways to arrange science fiction* = 5! = 120

*ways to arrange categories* = 3! = 6

(24)(720)(120)(6) = **12,441,600**

**23)**

**E.** All the points lie on the circle, so each line segment is a radius. The sum of the 4 lines will be 4 times the radius.

$r = \frac{75}{2} = 37.5$

$4r = \textbf{150}$

**24)**

**D.** Write a proportion and then solve for *x*.

$\frac{40}{45} = \frac{265}{x}$

$40x = 11,925$

$x = 298.125 \approx \textbf{298}$

**25)**

**D.** Find the amount of change and add to the original amount.

*amount of change* = *original amount* × *percent change*

= 37,500 × 0.055 = 2,062.50

37,500 + 2,062.50 = **$39,562.50**

**26)**

**E.** As shown in the figure, A can be placed inside, on, or outside the circle.

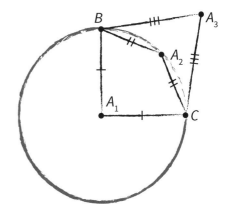

**27)**

**E.** Use the two sets of linear angles to find *b* and then *c*.

$a = b$

$a + b + 70 = 180$

$2a + 70 = 180$

$a = b = 55°$

$b + c = 180°$

$55 + c = 180$

$c = \mathbf{125°}$

**28)**

**C.** Plug each value into the equation.

$4(3 + 4)^2 - 4(3)^2 + 20 = 180 \neq 276$

$4(4 + 4)^2 - 4(3)^2 + 20 = 240 \neq 276$

$4(6 + 4)^2 - 4(6)^2 + 20 = \mathbf{276}$

$4(12 + 4)^2 - 4(12)^2 + 20 = 468 \neq 276$

$4(24 + 4)^2 - 4(24)^2 + 20 = 852 \neq 276$

**29)**

**C.** Plug 0 in for $x$ and solve for $y$.

$7y - 42x + 7 = 0$

$7y - 42(0) + 7 = 0$

$y = -1$

The $y$-intercept is at $\mathbf{(0, -1)}$.

**30)**

**A.** Use the midpoint formula to find the center of the circle and the distance formula to find its radius.

$M_x = \frac{4 + (-12)}{2} = -4$

$M_y = \frac{5 + (-11)}{2} = -3$

$M = (-4, -3)$

$r = \frac{1}{2}\sqrt{(4 - (-8))^2 + (5 - (-11))^2} = 10$

Use the center and radius to write the equation for the circle.

$(x - h)^2 + (y - k)^2 = r^2$

$\mathbf{(x + 4)^2 + (y + 3)^2 = 100}$

**31)**

**D.** {5, 11, 18, 20, **37**, 37, 60, 72, 90}

$median = 37$

$mode = 37$

$mean = \frac{60 + 5 + 18 + 20 + 37 + 37 + 11 + 90 + 72}{9} = 39$

**The median is less than the mean.**

**32)**

**D.** Use the volume to find the length of the cube's side.

$V = s^3$

$343 = s^3$

$s = 7$ m

Find the area of each side and multiply by 6 to find the total surface area.

$7(7) = 49$ m

$49(6) = \mathbf{294 \ m^2}$

**33)**

**E.** There are an infinite number of points with distance four from the origin, all of which lie on a circle centered at the origin with a radius of 4.

**34)**

**D.** Set up a system of equations and solve using elimination.

$f =$ the cost of a financial stock

$a =$ the cost of an auto stock

$50f + 10a = 1300$

$10f + 10a = 500$

$50f + 10a = 1300$

$+ -50f - 50a = -2500$

$-40a = -1,200$

$a = 30$

$50(30) = \mathbf{1,500}$

**35)**

**B.** Order the fractions by comparing the denominators.

$\frac{1}{2} > \frac{1}{3} > \frac{1}{7} > -\frac{1}{6} > -\frac{1}{5} > -\frac{1}{4}$

**36)**

**B.** Use the rules of exponents to simplify the expression.

$\frac{(3x^2y^2)^2}{3^3x^2y^3} = \frac{3^2x^4y^4}{3^3x^2y^3} = \frac{\mathbf{x^6y}}{\mathbf{3}}$

**37)**

**A.** A rotation of 180° is found by performing the transformation $(x, y) \rightarrow (-x, -y)$. Since this rotation is around the point A, treat point A as the origin.

A remains $\mathbf{(1, 1)}$.

$B$ is 4 units right and 2 units up from $A$, so count 4 units left and 2 units down from A to find $B'$: $(5,3) \rightarrow$ **(−3,−1)**

$C$ is 2 units right and 2 units up from $A$, so count 2 units left and 2 units down from $A$ to find $C'$: $(3,3) \rightarrow$ **(−1,−1)**

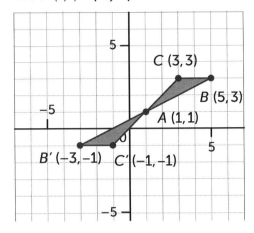

**38)**

**C.** Use the equation for exponential decay to find the year the population reached 1 million.

$y = a(1 - r)^t$

$y = 1250000(1 - 0.05)^t$

$1,000,000 = 1250000(1 - 0.05)^t$

$0.8 = 0.95^t$

$\log_{0.8} 0.8 = \log_{0.8} 0.95^t$

$1 = t \times \dfrac{\log 0.95}{\log .8}$

$t = 4.35$

**The population will reach 1 million in 2013.**

**39)**

**B.** Calculate the volume of water in tank A.

$V = l \times w \times h$

$5 \times 10 \times 1 = 50 \text{ ft}^3$

Find the height this volume would reach in tank B.

$V = l \times w \times h$

$50 = 5 \times 5 \times h$

$h = \textbf{2 ft}$

**40)**

**A.** Simplify each root and add.

$\sqrt[3]{64} = 4$

$\sqrt[3]{729} = 9$

$4 + 9 = \textbf{13}$

**41)**

**B.** Use the combination formula to find the number of ways to choose 2 people out of a group of 20.

$C(20,2) = \dfrac{20!}{2!\,18!} = \textbf{190}$

**42)**

**A.** Simplify the inequality.

$2x + 4 \geq 5x - 20 - 3x + 12$

$2x + 4 \geq 2x - 8$

$4 \geq -8$

Since the inequality is always true, the solution is all real numbers, $(-\infty, \infty)$.

**43)**

**B.** Add the corresponding parts of each matrix.

$$\begin{bmatrix} 6 & 4 \\ 8 & -2 \\ 5 & -3 \end{bmatrix} + \begin{bmatrix} -2 & 5 \\ 7 & 1 \\ -4 & 4 \end{bmatrix} = \begin{bmatrix} \mathbf{4} & \mathbf{9} \\ \mathbf{15} & \mathbf{-1} \\ \mathbf{1} & \mathbf{1} \end{bmatrix}$$

**44)**

**A.** Use the zeros of the function to find the intervals where it is less than 0.

$2x^2 - 4x - 6 = 0$

$(2x - 6)(x + 1) = 0$

$x = 3$ and $x = -1$

$(-\infty, -1) \rightarrow 2x^2 - 4x - 6 > 0$

$(-1, 3) \rightarrow 2x^2 - 4x - 6 < 0$

$(3, \infty) \rightarrow 2x^2 - 4x - 6 > 0$

The function is less than 0 on the interval **(−1,3)**.

**45)**

**B.** The altitude creates a **30–60–90 triangle with a height of $5\sqrt{3}$.**

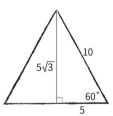

**46)**

**D.** Factor the equation and set each factor equal to 0.

$y = 16x^3 - 48x^2$

$16x^2(x - 3) = 0$

$x = 0$ and $x = 3$

## 47)

**B.** Use the formula for the determinant of a $2 \times 2$ matrix.

$|\mathbf{D}| = ad - bc$

$= 3(9) - 7(4) = -1$

## 48)

**C.** Make sure there are no factors that cancel, and then set the denominator equal to 0.

$$\frac{x^3 - 16x}{-4x^2 + 4x + 24} = \frac{x(x^2 - 16)}{-4(x^2 - x - 6)}$$

$$= \frac{x(x+4)(x-4)}{-4(x-3)(x+2)}$$

The graph has no holes.

$-4(x - 3)(x + 2) = 0$

$x = 3$ and $x = -2$

## 49)

**D.** Find the perimeter of $\triangle JKL$.

$P = 10 + 18.2 + 13.4 = 41.6$

Find the scale factor between the two triangles.

$\frac{QR}{KL} = \frac{47.1}{18.2} = 2.588$

Multiply the perimeter of $\triangle JKL$ by the scale factor to find the perimeter of $\triangle PQR$.

$(2.588)(41.6) = 107.6 \approx 108$

## 50)

**B.** Find the sum of the 13 numbers whose mean is 30.

$13 \times 30 = 390$

Find the sum of the 8 numbers whose mean is 42.

$8 \times 42 = 336$

Find the sum and mean of the remaining 5 numbers.

$390 - 336 = 54$

$\frac{54}{5} = 10.8$

# seven

# PRACTICE TEST TWO

**Directions: Read the problem carefully, and choose the best answer.**

**1)** Simplify: $\frac{3}{2-i}$

   **A.** $2 + i$

   **B.** $6 + 3i$

   **C.** $\frac{2+i}{5}$

   **D.** $\frac{6+3i}{5}$

   **E.** $\frac{3}{2} - \frac{3}{i}$

**2)** The coordinates of point $A$ are $(7, 12)$ and the coordinates of point $C$ are $(-3, 10)$. If $C$ is the midpoint of $\overline{AB}$, what are the coordinates of point $B$?

   **A.** $(-13, 8)$

   **B.** $(-13, 11)$

   **C.** $(2, 11)$

   **D.** $(2, 14)$

   **E.** $(17, 14)$

**3)** Simplify: $(4.71 \times 10^3) - (2.98 \times 10^2)$

   **A.** $1.73 \times 10$

   **B.** $4.412 \times 10^2$

   **C.** $1.73 \times 10^3$

   **D.** $-14.038 \times 10^5$

   **E.** $4.412 \times 10^3$

**4)** A restaurant offers burritos on a corn or a flour tortilla, 5 types of meat, 6 types of cheese, and 3 different toppings. When ordering, customers can choose 1 type of tortilla, 1 meat, and 1 cheese. They can then add any of the 3 toppings. How many different burrito combinations are possible?

   **A.** 180

   **B.** 330

   **C.** 480

   **D.** 660

   **E.** 1620

**5)** A cube is inscribed in a sphere such that each vertex on the cube touches the sphere. If the volume of the sphere is $972\pi$ cm³, what is the approximate volume of the cube in cubic centimeters?

   **A.** 9

   **B.** 104

   **C.** 927

   **D.** 1125

   **E.** 1729

**6)** If $16^{x+10} = 8^{3x}$, what is the value of $x$?

   **A.** 0.5

   **B.** 2

   **C.** 4

   **D.** 5

   **E.** 8

**7)** What is the total number of 6-digit numbers in which each individual digit is less than 3 or greater than 6?

   **A.** 38,880

   **B.** 46,656

   **C.** 80,452

   **D.** 101,370

   **E.** 279,936

**8)** Simplify: $(1.2 \times 10^{-3})(1.13 \times 10^{-4})$

   **A.** $1.356 \times 10^{-12}$

   **B.** $1.356 \times 10^{-7}$

   **C.** $1.356 \times 10^{-1}$

   **D.** $1.356 \times 10$

   **E.** $1.356 \times 10^{12}$

**9)** Which of the following is equivalent to $54z^4 + 18z^3 + 3z + 3$?

   **A.** $18z^4 + 6z^3 + z + 1$

   **B.** $3z(18z^3 + 6z^2 + 1)$

   **C.** $3(18z^4 + 6z^3 + z + 1)$

   **D.** $72z^7 + 3z$

   **E.** $54(z^4 + 18z^3 + 3z + 3)$

**10)** Which of the following represents a linear equation?

   **A.** $\sqrt[3]{y} = x$

   **B.** $\sqrt[3]{x} = y$

   **C.** $\sqrt[3]{y} = x^2$

   **D.** $y = \sqrt[6]{x^3}$

   **E.** $y = \sqrt[3]{x^3}$

**11)** Which of the angles in the figure below are congruent?

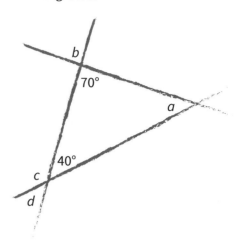

   **A.** $a$ and $d$

   **B.** $b$ and $d$

   **C.** $a$ and $b$

   **D.** $c$ and $b$

   **E.** $c$ and $a$

**12)** What is the $x$-intercept of the given equation?

$10x + 10y = 10$

   **A.** $(1, 0)$

   **B.** $(0, 1)$

   **C.** $(0, 0)$

   **D.** $(1, 1)$

   **E.** $(10, 10)$

**13)** Two spheres are tangent to each other. One has a volume of $36\pi$, and the other has a volume of $288\pi$. What is the greatest distance between a point on one of the spheres and a point on the other sphere?

   **A.** 6

   **B.** 9

   **C.** 18

   **D.** 36

   **E.** 63

**14)** What is the slope of the graph below?

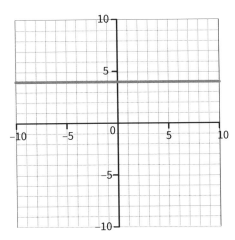

A. ∞

B. Nonexistent

C. 0

D. 1

E. 4

**15)** Cone *A* is similar to cone *B* with a scale factor of 3:4. If the volume of cone *A* is 54π, what is the volume of cone *B*?

A. 72π

B. 128π

C. 162π

D. 216π

E. 378π

**16)** The line of best fit is calculated for a data set that tracks the number of miles that passenger cars traveled annually in the US from 1960 to 2010. In the model, $x = 0$ represents the year 1960, and $y$ is the number of miles traveled in billions. If the line of best fit is $y = 0.0293x + 0.563$, approximately how many additional miles were traveled for every 5 years that passed?

A. 0.0293 billion

B. 0.1465 billion

C. 0.5630 billion

D. 0.7100 billion

E. 2.9615 billion

**17)** Simplify: $(3^2 \div 1^3) - (4 - 8^2) + 2^4$

A. −35

B. −4

C. 9

D. 28

E. 85

**18)** Find the approximate value of *x* in the triangle below.

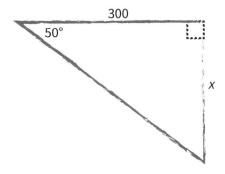

A. 77

B. 229

C. 300

D. 357

E. 400

**19)** Which of the following series of transformations does NOT preserve congruency of both sides and angles in a shape on the coordinate plane?

A. Reflect across the line $y = x$, and then translate 3 units left.

B. Rotate 90° clockwise about the origin, and then reflect across the x-axis.

C. Reflect across the x-axis, and then dilate by a factor of 3.

D. Translate 2 units right, reflect about the y-axis, and then rotate 60° in a clockwise direction.

E. Rotate 180° counterclockwise about the origin, and then translate 4 units to the right.

20) Simplify: $\dfrac{5^2(3)+3(-2)^2}{4+3^2-2(5-8)}$

A. $\dfrac{9}{8}$

B. $\dfrac{63}{19}$

C. $\dfrac{87}{19}$

D. $9$

E. $\dfrac{21}{2}$

21) If $y = 2x^2 + 12x - 3$ is written if the form $y = a(x - h)^2 + k$, what is the value of $k$?

A. $-2$

B. $-3$

C. $-15$

D. $-18$

E. $-21$

22) What are the roots of the function $f(x) = 4x^2 - 6x + 7$?

A. $\left\{\dfrac{3+i\sqrt{19}}{4}, \dfrac{3-i\sqrt{19}}{4}\right\}$

B. $\{0, 2\}$

C. $\left\{\dfrac{6+\sqrt{-76}}{4}, \dfrac{6-\sqrt{76}}{4}\right\}$

D. $\left\{\dfrac{3+i\sqrt{5}}{4}, \dfrac{3-i\sqrt{5}}{4}\right\}$

E. $\left\{\dfrac{3+\sqrt{19}}{4}, \dfrac{3-\sqrt{19}}{4}\right\}$

23) Which of the following is the vertical asymptote of the function

$f(x) = \dfrac{x+4}{-2x-6}$?

A. $x = -6$

B. $x = -3$

C. $y = -2$

D. $y = \dfrac{1}{2}$

E. $x = 3$

24) If one leg of a right triangle has a length of 40, which of the following could be the lengths of the two remaining sides?

A. 50 and 41

B. 9 and 41

C. 9 and 30

D. 50 and 63

E. 41 and 63

25) Simplify: $\dfrac{12!2!}{10!3!}$

A. 22

B. 44

C. 66

D. 88

E. 121

26) What transformation is created by the $-3$ in the graph of $y = -3|x - 2| + 2$?

A. The $-3$ moves the vertex down 3 and reflects the graph over the $x$-axis.

B. The $-3$ moves the vertex to the left 3 and widens the graph.

C. The $-3$ makes the graph wider and reflects it over the $x$-axis.

D. The $-3$ makes the graph narrower and reflects the graph over the $x$-axis.

E. The $-3$ moves the vertex to the left and narrows the graph.

**27)** Which of the following statements must be true for triangle *ABC*?

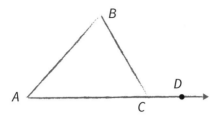

I. $AC + CB > AB$
II. $m\angle BCD = m\angle A + m\angle B$
III. $m\angle BCD + m\angle BCA = 90°$
IV. $m\angle A = m\angle C$

A. I only
B. II only
C. I and II
D. II and IV
E. I, II, and III

**28)** A company interviewed 21 applicants for a recent opening. Of these applicants, 7 wore blue and 6 wore white, while 5 applicants wore both blue and white. What is the number of applicants who wore neither blue nor white?

A. 1
B. 6
C. 8
D. 12
E. 13

**29)** If $\frac{4x-5}{3} = \frac{\frac{1}{2}(2-6)}{5}$, what is the value of *x*?

A. $-\frac{2}{7}$
B. $-\frac{4}{17}$
C. $\frac{16}{17}$
D. 1
E. $\frac{8}{7}$

**30)** A wedge from a cylindrical piece of cheese was cut as shown. If the entire wheel of cheese weighed 73 pounds before the wedge was removed, what is the approximate remaining weight of the cheese?

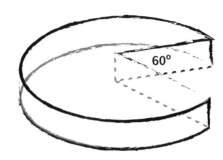

A. 12.17 pounds
B. 37.00 pounds
C. 55.00 pounds
D. 60.83 pounds
E. 66.92 pounds

**31)** What is the value of *z* in the following system?

$z - 2x = 14$
$2z - 6x = 18$

A. −7
B. −2
C. 3
D. 5
E. 24

**32)** If a student answers 42 out of 48 questions correctly on a quiz, what percentage of questions did she answer correctly?

A. 82.5%
B. 85%
C. 86%
D. 87.5%
E. 90%

**33)** What is the approximate value of $a$ in the triangle below if $b$ is $\frac{7}{8}$ the value of $a$?

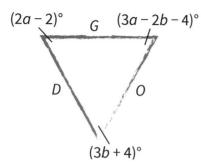

$(2a-2)°$  G  $(3a-2b-4)°$

D     O

$(3b+4)°$

A.  22

B.  28

C.  31

D.  42

E.  60

**34)** A worker was paid $15,036 for 7 months of work. If he received the same amount each month, how much was he paid for the first 2 months?

A.  $2,148

B.  $4,296

C.  $5,137

D.  $6,444

E.  $8,592

**35)** The population of a town was 7,250 in 2014 and 7,375 in 2015. What was the percent increase from 2014 to 2015 to the nearest tenth of a percent?

A.  1.5%

B.  1.6%

C.  1.7%

D.  1.8%

E.  2.0%

**36)** Which of the following is a solution to the inequality $2x + y \le -10$?

A.  $(0, 0)$

B.  $(10, 2)$

C.  $(10, 10)$

D.  $(-10, -10)$

E.  $(0, 10)$

**37)** A bag contains 6 blue, 8 silver, and 4 green marbles. Two marbles are drawn from the bag. What is the probability that the second marble drawn will be green if replacement is not allowed?

A.  $\frac{2}{51}$

B.  $\frac{2}{9}$

C.  $\frac{4}{17}$

D.  $\frac{11}{17}$

E.  $\frac{7}{9}$

**38)** What is the approximate diagonal length of square QTSR shown in the figure below?

A.  3.0

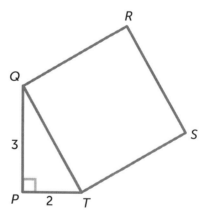

R

Q

3

S

P   2   T

B.  3.6

C.  4.0

D.  5.1

E.  13.0

**39)** What are the real zero(s) of the following polynomial?

$2n^2 + 2n - 12 = 0$

**A.** $\{-3, 2\}$

**B.** $\{2\}$

**C.** $\{2, 0\}$

**D.** $\{2, 4\}$

**E.** There are no real zeros of $n$.

**40)** In the following graph of $f(x) = y$, for how many values of $x$ does $|f(x)| = 1$?

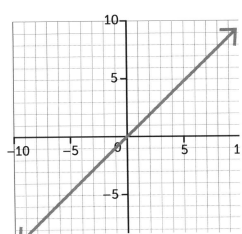

**A.** 0

**B.** 1

**C.** 2

**D.** 4

**E.** ∞

**41)** Simplify: $\left(\frac{4x^{-3}y^4z}{8x^{-5}y^3z^{-2}}\right)^2$

**A.** $\frac{x^4yz^3}{2}$

**B.** $\frac{x^4y^2z^6}{2}$

**C.** $\frac{x^4y^2z^6}{4}$

**D.** $\frac{x^4yz^3}{4}$

**E.** $\frac{x^4y^2z^6}{8}$

**42)** If the surface area of a cylinder with radius of 4 feet is $48\pi$ square feet, what is its volume?

**A.** $1\pi$ ft.$^3$

**B.** $16\pi$ ft.$^3$

**C.** $32\pi$ ft.$^3$

**D.** $48\pi$ ft.$^3$

**E.** $64\pi$ ft.$^3$

**43)** If the water in a reservoir decreases every day by 4%, by how much will the water decrease over a 7-day week?

**A.** 24.9%

**B.** 28.0%

**C.** 32.4%

**D.** 96.0%

**E.** 131.6%

**44)** If $B = \begin{bmatrix} 6 & 4 \\ 8 & -2 \\ 5 & -3 \end{bmatrix}$ and $C = \begin{bmatrix} -2 & 5 \\ 7 & 1 \\ -4 & 4 \end{bmatrix}$, find $B - C$.

**A.** $\begin{bmatrix} 8 & -1 \\ 1 & -1 \\ 9 & 1 \end{bmatrix}$

**B.** $\begin{bmatrix} 4 & -1 \\ 1 & -3 \\ 1 & -7 \end{bmatrix}$

**C.** $\begin{bmatrix} 8 & -1 \\ 1 & -3 \\ 9 & -7 \end{bmatrix}$

**D.** $\begin{bmatrix} 4 & -1 \\ 1 & -1 \\ 1 & 1 \end{bmatrix}$

**E.** These matrices cannot be subtracted.

**45)** Find $(f - g)(x)$ if $f(x) = x^2 + 16x$ and $g(x) = 5x^2 + 4x + 25$.

**A.** $-4x^2 + 12x - 25$

**B.** $-4x^2 - 12x - 25$

**C.** $-4x^2 - 20x + 25$

**D.** $4x^2 - 20x - 25$

**E.** $4x^2 + 12x - 25$

46) Which of the following is listed in order from least to greatest?

A. $-0.95, 0, \frac{2}{5}, 0.35, \frac{3}{4}$

B. $-1, -\frac{1}{10}, -0.11, \frac{5}{6}, 0.75$

C. $-\frac{3}{4}, -0.2, 0, \frac{2}{3}, 0.55$

D. $-1.1, -\frac{4}{5}, -0.13, 0.7, \frac{9}{11}$

E. $-0.0001, -\frac{1}{12}, 0, \frac{2}{3}, \frac{4}{5}$

47) What is the measure of each exterior angle of a regular 300-gon?

A. $1.2°$

B. $2.4°$

C. $178.8°$

D. $300°$

E. $360°$

48) Simplify: $\frac{3+\sqrt{3}}{4-\sqrt{3}}$

A. $\frac{13}{15}$

B. $-\frac{1}{4}$

C. $\frac{15+7\sqrt{3}}{13}$

D. $\frac{15}{19}$

E. $\frac{15+7\sqrt{3}}{19}$

49) If the smallest angle in a non-right triangle is 20° and the shortest side is 14, what is the length of the longest side if the largest angle is 100°?

A. 12.78

B. 34.31

C. 40.31

D. 70.02

E. 127.81

50) New York had the fewest months with less than 3 inches of rain in every year except:

### Number of Months with 3 or Fewer Than 3 Inches of Rain

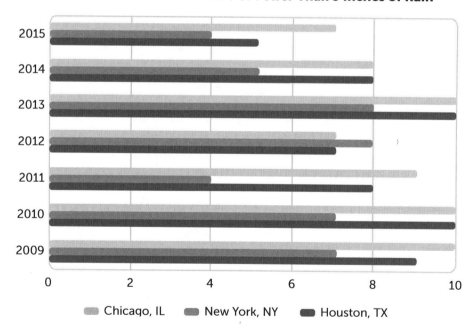

A. 2011

B. 2012

C. 2013

D. 2014

E. 2015

# ANSWER KEY

**1)**

**D.** Multiply by the complex conjugate and simplify.

$\frac{3}{2-i}$

Multiply: $\left(\frac{3}{2-i}\right)\left(\frac{2+i}{2+i}\right)$

$\frac{3(2+i)}{4-2i+2i-i^2}$

$= \frac{3(2+i)}{4-(-1)}$

$= \frac{(6+3i)}{5}$

**2)**

**A.** Use the midpoint formula to find point $B$.

$M_x: \frac{(7+x)}{2} = -3$

$x = -13$

$M_y: \frac{(12+y)}{2} = 10$

$y = 8$

$B = (-13, 8)$

**3)**

**E.** Make the exponents the same and subtract the digit parts of each term.

$(4.71 \times 10^3) - (2.98 \times 10^2)$

$4.71 \times 10 \times 10^2 = 47.1 \times 10^2$

$47.1 - 2.98 = 44.12$

$44.12 \times 10^2 = \textbf{4.412} \times \textbf{10}^3$

**4)**

**C.** Use the fundamental counting principle. Each topping has two possible choices (yes or no).

$2(5)(6)(2)(2)(2) = \textbf{480}$

**5)**

**D.** Use the formula for the volume of a sphere to find its radius.

$V = \frac{4}{3}\pi r^3$

$972\pi = \frac{4}{3}\pi r^3$

$r = 9$

Use the super Pythagorean theorem to find the side of the cube.

$d^2 = a^2 + b^2 + c^2$

$18^2 = 3s^2$

$s \approx 10.4$

Use the length of the side to find the volume of the cube.

$V = s^3$

$V \approx (10.4)^3$

$V \approx \textbf{1125}$

**6)**

**E.** Rewrite the bases so they are the same, then set the exponents equal and solve.

$16^{x+10} = 8^{3x}$

$(2^4)^{x+10} = (2^3)^{3x}$

$2^{4x+40} = 2^{9x}$

$4x + 40 = 9x$

$\textbf{\textit{x} = 8}$

**7)**

**A.** There are six digits that can be used to make up the 6-digit number: 0, 1, 2, 7, 8, and 9. However, 0 cannot be used for the first digit.

Use the fundamental counting principle: (5)(6)(6)(6)(6)(6) = **38,880**.

**8)**

---

**B.** Multiply the digits and add the exponents.

$(1.2 \times 10^{-3})(1.13 \times 10^{-4})$

$1.2 \times 1.13 = 1.356$

$-3 + (-4) = -7$

**$1.356 \times 10^{-7}$**

**9)**

---

**C.** Factor the expression using the greatest common factor of 3.

$54z^4 + 18z^3 + 3z + 3 =$

**$3(18z^4 + 6z^3 + z + 1)$**

**10)**

---

**E.** Solve each equation for $y$ and find the equation with a power of 1.

$\sqrt[3]{y} = x \rightarrow y = x^3$

$\sqrt[3]{x} = y \rightarrow y = \sqrt[3]{x}$

$\sqrt[3]{y} = x^2 \rightarrow y = x^6$

$y = \sqrt[6]{x^3} \rightarrow y = x^{1/2}$

$y = \sqrt[3]{x^3} \rightarrow$ **$y = x$**

**11)**

---

**C.** Find the measure of each angle.

$m\angle a = 180 - (70 + 40) = 70°$

$m\angle b = 70°$

$m\angle c = 180 - 40 = 140°$

$m\angle d = 40°$

**$\angle a \cong \angle b$**

**12)**

---

**A.** Plug 0 in for $y$ and solve for $x$.

$10x + 10y = 10$

$10x + 10(0) = 10$

$x = 1$

The $x$-intercept is at **$(1, 0)$**.

**13)**

---

**C.** The greatest distance will be between two points at opposite ends of each sphere's diameters. Find the diameter of each sphere and add them.

$36\pi = \frac{4}{3}\pi r_1^3$

$r_1 = 3$

$d_1 = 2(3) = 6$

$288\pi = \frac{4}{3}\pi r_2^3$

$r_2 = 6$

$d_2 = 2(6) = 12$

$d_1 + d_1 = 6 + 12 = $ **18**

**14)**

---

**C.** The slope of a horizontal line is always 0.

**15)**

---

**B.** Set up a proportion. Cube the scale factor when calculating volume.

$\frac{54\pi}{x} = \frac{3^3}{4^3}$

**$x = 128\pi$**

**16)**

---

**B.** The slope 0.0293 gives the increase in passenger car miles (in billions) for each year that passes. Muliply this value by 5 to find the increase that occurs over 5 years: 5(0.0293) = **0.1465 billion miles**.

**17)**

---

**E.** Simplify using PEMDAS.

$(3^2 \div 1^3) - (4 - 8^2) + 2^4$

$= (9 \div 1) - (4 - 64) + 16$

$= 9 - (-60) + 16 = $ **85**

**18)**

---

**D.** Use the equation for tangent.

$\tan 50° = \frac{x}{300}$

$x = 300(\tan 50°)$

**$x \approx 357$**

**19)**

---

**C.** Reflections, rotations, and translations always preserve congruency of shapes in a plane. A dilation preserves angles but not side lengths.

**20)**

---

**C.** Simplify using PEMDAS.

$\frac{5^2(3) + 3(-2)^2}{4 + 3^2 - 2(5 - 8)}$

$= \frac{5^2(3) + 3(-2)^2}{4 + 3^2 - 2(-3)}$

$= \frac{25(3) + 3(4)}{4 + 9 - 2(-3)}$

$$= \frac{75+12}{13+6} = \frac{87}{19}$$

**When $a$ is negative, the graph is reflected over the $x$-axis.**

**21)**

**E.** Complete the square to put the quadratic equation in vertex form.

$y = 2x^2 + 12x - 3$

$y = 2(x^2 + 6x + \underline{\hspace{1cm}}) - 3 + \underline{\hspace{1cm}}$

$y = 2(x^2 + 6x + 9) - 3 - 18$

$\mathbf{y = 2(x + 3)2 - 21}$

**22)**

**A.** Use the quadratic formula.

$f(x) = 4x^2 - 6x + 7$

$x = \frac{-(-6) \pm \sqrt{(-6)^2 - 4(4)(7)}}{2(4)}$

$\mathbf{x = \frac{3 \pm i\sqrt{19}}{4}}$

**23)**

**B.** Find where the denominator equals 0.

$-2x - 6 = 0$

$\mathbf{x = -3}$

**24)**

**B.** Use the Pythagorean theorem to determine which set of values forms a right triangle.

$40^2 + 41^2 = 50^2$

$3,281 \ne 2,500$

$9^2 + 40^2 = 41^2$

$\mathbf{1,681 = 1,681}$

$9^2 + 30^2 = 40^2$

$981 \ne 1,600$

$40^2 + 50^2 = 63^2$

$4,100 \ne 3,969$

$40^2 + 41^2 = 63^2$

$3,281 \ne 3,969$

**25)**

**B.** Cancel terms that appear on the top and bottom, and then mulitply.

$\frac{12!\,2!}{10!\,3!}$

$= \frac{12 \times 11 \times 10! \times 2 \times 1}{10! \times 3 \times 2 \times 1}$

$= \frac{132}{3} = \mathbf{44}$

**26)**

**D.** For the function $y = a|x - h| + k$:

**When $|a| > 1$, the graph will narrow.**

**27)**

**B.** I. True: The sum of any two sides of a triangle must always be greater than the third side.

II. True: The exterior angle of a triangle is always equal to the sum of the opposite interior angles.

III. False: $\angle BCD$ and $\angle BCA$ are a linear pair, so they sum to 180°, not 90°.

IV. False: This cannot be determined from the information in the figure.

**28)**

**E.** Set up an equation to find the number of people wearing neither white nor blue. Subtract the number of people wearing both colors so they are not counted twice.

$21 = 7 + 6 + neither - 5$

$neither = \mathbf{13}$

**29)**

**C.** Cross multiply and solve for x.

$\frac{4x-5}{3} = \frac{\frac{1}{2}(2x-6)}{5}$

$5(4x - 5) = \frac{3}{2}(2x - 6)$

$20x - 25 = 3x - 9$

$17x = 16$

$x = \frac{16}{17}$

**30)**

**D.** Set up a proportion to find the weight of the removed wedge.

$\frac{60°}{x\,lb.} = \frac{360°}{73\,lb.}$

$x \approx 12.17\,lb.$

Subtract the removed wedge from the whole to find the weight of the remaining piece.

$73 - 12.17 = \mathbf{60.83}$

**31)**

**E.** Solve the system using substitution.

$z - 2x = 14 \rightarrow z = 2x + 14$

$2z - 6x = 18$

$2(2x + 14) - 6x = 18$

$4x + 28 - 6x = 18$

$-2x = -10$

$x = 5$

$z - 2(5) = 14$

$z = 24$

## 32)

**D.** Use the formula for percentages.

$percent = \dfrac{part}{whole}$

$= \dfrac{42}{48}$

$= 0.875 = \textbf{87.5\%}$

## 33)

**C.** Write a system of equations and solve using substitution.

$5a + b - 2 = 180$

$b = \dfrac{7}{8}a$

$5a + \dfrac{7}{8}a - 2 = 180$

$a \approx \textbf{31}$

## 34)

**B.** Write a proportion and then solve for $x$.

$\dfrac{15{,}036}{7} = \dfrac{x}{2}$

$7x = 30{,}072$

$x = \textbf{4,296}$

## 35)

**C.** Use the formula for percent change.

$percent\ change = \dfrac{amount\ of\ change}{original\ amount}$

$= \dfrac{(7{,}375 - 7{,}250)}{7{,}250} = 0.017 = \textbf{1.7\%}$

## 36)

**D.** Plug in each set of values and determine if the inequality is true.

$2(0) + 0 \le -10$ FALSE

$2(10) + 2 \le -10$ FALSE

$2(10) + 10 \le -10$ FALSE

$2(-10) + (-10) \le -10$ TRUE

$2(0) + 10 \le -10$ FALSE

## 37)

**B.** Find the probability that the second marble will be green if the first marble is blue, silver, or green, and then add these probabilities together.

$P$(first blue and second green) = $P$(blue) × $P$(green|first blue) = $\dfrac{6}{18} \times \dfrac{4}{17} = \dfrac{4}{51}$

$P$(first silver and second green) = $P$(silver) × $P$(green|first silver) = $\dfrac{8}{18} \times \dfrac{4}{17} = \dfrac{16}{153}$

$P$(first green and second green) = $P$(green) × $P$(green|first green) = $\dfrac{4}{18} \times \dfrac{3}{17} = \dfrac{2}{51}$

$P$(second green) = $\dfrac{4}{51} + \dfrac{16}{153} + \dfrac{2}{51} = \dfrac{2}{9}$

## 38)

**D.** Find the hypotenuse of $\Delta QPT$.

$H_1 = QT = \sqrt{3^2 + 2^2} = 3.6$

Find the diagonal of $QRST$.

$H_1 = SQ = \sqrt{3.6^2 + 3.6^2} = \textbf{5.1}$

## 39)

**A.** Factor the trinomial and set each factor equal to 0.

$2n^2 + 2n - 12 = 0$

$2(n^2 + n - 6) = 0$

$2(n + 3)(n - 2) = 0$

$\boldsymbol{n = -3}$ and $\boldsymbol{n = 2}$

## 40)

**C.** The absolute value of $f(x)$ equals 1 twice: once in quadrant I and once in quadrant III.

## 41)

**C.** Use the rules of exponents to simplify the expression.

$$\left( \dfrac{4x^{-3}y^4z}{8x^{-5}y^3z^{-2}} \right)^2 = \left( \dfrac{x^2yz^3}{2} \right)^2 = \dfrac{x^4y^2z^6}{4}$$

## 42)

**C.** Find the height of the cylinder using the equation for surface area.

$SA = 2\pi rh + 2\pi r^2$

$48\pi = 2\pi(4)h + 2\pi(4)^2$

$h = 2$

Find the volume using the volume equation.

$V = \pi r^2 h$

$V = \pi(4)^2(2) = \textbf{32}\boldsymbol{\pi}\ \textbf{ft.}^3$

## 43)

**A.** Use the exponential decay function. The value $\dfrac{y}{a}$ represents the percent of the water remaining.

$y = a(1 - r)^t$

$y = (1 - 0.04)^7$

$y = (0.96)^7 = 0.751$

After 7 days, the new amount of water is 0.751, or 75.1% of the original amount. It has decreased by 100 − 75.1 = **24.9%**.

**44)**

**C.** Subtract the corresponding parts of each matrix.

$$\begin{bmatrix} 6 & 4 \\ 8 & -2 \\ 5 & -3 \end{bmatrix} - \begin{bmatrix} -2 & 5 \\ 7 & 1 \\ -4 & 4 \end{bmatrix} = \begin{bmatrix} \mathbf{8} & \mathbf{-1} \\ \mathbf{1} & \mathbf{-3} \\ \mathbf{9} & \mathbf{-7} \end{bmatrix}$$

**45)**

**A.** Subtract $g(x)$ from $f(x)$.

$x^2 + 16x - (5x^2 + 4x + 25) = x^2 + 16x - 5x^2 - 4x - 25 = \mathbf{-4x^2 + 12x - 25}$

**46)**

**D.** Write each value in decimal form and compare.

$-0.95 < 0 < 0.4 < 0.35 < 0.75$
FALSE

$-1 < -0.1 < -0.11 < 0.8\overline{3} < 0.75$
FALSE

$-0.75 < -0.2 < 0 < 0.\overline{66} < 0.55$
FALSE

$-1.1 < -0.8 < -0.13 < 0.7 < 0.\overline{81}$
TRUE

$-0.0001 < -0.\overline{83} < 0 < 0.\overline{66} < 0.8$
FALSE

**47)**

**A.** **Correct.** The sum of all the exterior angles of a regular $n$-gon is always 360°. Because there are 300 vertices in a 300-gon, the exterior angle at each vertex is $\frac{360}{300} = \mathbf{1.2°}$.

**48)**

**C.** Multiply by the complex conjugate and simplify.

$$\frac{3 + \sqrt{3}}{4 - \sqrt{3}} \left( \frac{4 + \sqrt{3}}{4 + \sqrt{3}} \right)$$

$$= \frac{12 + 4\sqrt{3} + 3\sqrt{3} + 3}{16 - 4\sqrt{3} + 4\sqrt{3} - 3} = \frac{\mathbf{15 + 7\sqrt{3}}}{\mathbf{13}}$$

**49)**

**C.** Use the law of sines.

$$\frac{\sin 20°}{14} = \frac{\sin 100°}{x}$$

$$x = \frac{14(\sin 100°)}{\sin 20°}$$

$$x = \mathbf{40.31}$$

**50)**

**B.** In 2012, New York had more months with less than 3 inches of rain than either Chicago or Houston.